# Sustaining Our Forests

*A Blueprint for Environmental and Economic Harmony*

By

## Evaristus Chukwugoziem Okonkwo

Sustaining our forests ©copyright 2023 Evaristus Chukwugoziem Okonkwo

-2-



Obasi Reloaded Publishing Inc.

ISBN: 9798861060998

Imprint: independently published

First edition: 2023

Printed in the United States of America.

Cover design by Oko Obasi

# CONTENTS

Dedication

Acknowledgement

Preface

Chapter 5: Social and Cultural Aspects

- Indigenous knowledge and forest management

- The role of local communities

- Lessons from global forest stewardship models

Chapter 6: Lessons from Global Models

- Case studies of successful sustainable forestry practices

- The impact of international agreements (e.g., FSC certification)

- Adaptation of global models to Nigeria

Chapter 7: Nigeria's Forests and the Anambra State Context

- An overview of Nigeria's forest resources

- The unique challenges facing Anambra State

- The interconnectedness of forests and water resources

Chapter 8: Challenges and Threats to Anambra's Forests

- Deforestation drivers in the state

- The impact of agricultural expansion

- Logging and illegal activities

Chapter 9: Strategies for Sustainable Forest Management in Anambra State

- Local community involvement and empowerment

- Reforestation and afforestation programs

- Promoting sustainable agricultural practices

Chapter 10: Policy and Governance

- The role of government in sustainable forestry

- Legal frameworks and enforcement

- The importance of cross-sectoral collaboration


Chapter 11: The Economic Potential of Sustainable Forestry in Anambra State

- Economic benefits of sustainable forest management

- The role of eco-tourism

- Case studies of successful initiatives

Chapter 12: Education and Awareness

- The need for public awareness campaigns

- Environmental education in schools

- Building a culture of forest conservation

Chapter 13: Challenges and Solutions

- Overcoming resistance to change

- Addressing short-term economic pressures

- Mobilizing resources for implementation

Chapter 14: Monitoring and Evaluation

- Developing forest health indicators

- Tracking progress toward sustainability goals

- The role of technology in monitoring

Chapter 15: Green and Sustainable Yield Goals

- The significance of adopting green yield goals for Anambra State's forests

- A call to action for all stakeholders to embrace and implement green and sustainable yield practices in the preservation and management of Anambra's vital forest resources.

Epilogue

Glossary of key terms

References

Additional resources for further reading

Contact information for relevant organizations and agencies.

About the author

# Dedication

This book, "Sustaining our Forests," is dedicated to the memory of the People who have tragically lost their lives due to insecurity and floods caused by deforestation. May their spirits find solace in the preservation of our natural world.

In addition, this dedication extends to all the forest officers and guards who have gone to be with the LORD, having devoted their lives to the protection and conservation of our forests. Their unwavering commitment to safeguarding our environment is a legacy that will forever inspire our efforts in maintaining the balance between human development and nature's well-being.

May their memory serve as a reminder of the urgent need to continue the fight for sustainable forests, not only for ourselves but for generations to come.

# ACKNOWLEDGEMENT

I would like to extend my heartfelt gratitude to the following individuals, whose unwavering support and invaluable contributions have been instrumental in the creation of my book, "Sustaining our Forests." Their dedication to the cause of preserving our natural resources and their support in my life have played a crucial role in this endeavor:

1. Prof Charles Chukwuma Soludo, CFR- The Executive Governor of Anambra State.

- Your exemplary work standards and policy implementation have been a profound source of inspiration in my quest to write about sustainable forests. Your ability to collaborate seamlessly with elected officials is commendable and has enriched the content of this book.

2. Senator Dr. Patrick Ifeanyi Uba (CON)- Senator representing Anambra South in the National Assembly.

- Your unwavering support, particularly in matters related to security in the state and environmental conservation, has been a cornerstone of my research. Your quality representation in the Senate has strengthened the message of this book.

3. Hon Uchenna Eleodimmuo- Member representing Nnewi North, Nnewi South, and Ekwusigo Federal Constituency

- Your proactive efforts towards the betterment of our community, especially in environmental sustainability, have provided invaluable insights for this book. Your commitment is evident in these pages.

4. Hon Augustine Onyekachukwu Ike- Member representing Nnewi North in the Anambra State House of Assembly

- Your presence in Anambra State House of Assembly and the support you've received from our Governor have contributed significantly to the discourse on sustainable forests in our region. Your involvement is greatly appreciated.

5. Engr Dr. Felix Odimegwu- Commissioner of Environment

- Your care, support, and accessibility throughout the research process have been instrumental. Your expertise in environmental matters has enriched the content of this book.

6. Prof Offornze Amucheazi - Commissioner of Lands

- Your insights and commitment to sustainability have reshaped my perspective on land management, a vital aspect of forest conservation. Your contribution is evident in these pages.

7. Hon Amala Anazodo - Former Nnewi North House of Assembly Member

- Your enduring contributions both in Nnewi and during your tenure in the Assembly continue to resonate. Thank you for your service.

8. Hon Sir Melie Onyejepu - Former Director, Bureau of Public Procurement, Anambra State

- Your contributions to the betterment of Anambra are unforgettable. Thank you for your dedication.

9. Ngozi Anuli Iwouno, Esq. - Permanent Secretary, Ministry of Environment

- Your leadership has placed our ministry in the spotlight for its achievements and positive impact. Thank you for your excellent work.

10. Mrs. Achugamonye Onyinye- Head of Forestry Department, Ministry of Environment, Awka.

- Your commitment and intervention have been instrumental in preserving the Forestry Department. Thank you for your dedication.

11. Dr. Jacinta Ezenwenyi - Head of Forestry Department, Nnamdi Azikiwe University, Awka

- Your dedication in creating a conducive and practical learning environment is greatly appreciated by your staff and students.

12. Mr. Onyekachi Chukwu - Forestry Department Lecturer, Nnamdi Azikiwe University, Awka

- Thank you for your tireless efforts within the department and your commitment to sustainable forestry practices.

Special Mention:

- My wife, Mrs. Chinenye Juliet Okonkwo: Your unwavering love and support have sustained me throughout this writing journey. Your belief in this project has been a driving force.

- My Brother, Rev Fr. Kyrian K. Okonkwo, and my Sister, Dr. Chioma M. Okonkwo: Your constant encouragement and support have been a source of strength.

This book, "Sustaining our Forests," stands as a testament to the collaborative efforts of these individuals and their dedication to the cause of environmental preservation. I am profoundly grateful for their contributions and unwavering support.

**Evaristus Chukwugoziem Okonkwo**
Nnewi, Anambra State
Nigeria
September, 2023

# PREFACE

Forests have long held a special place in the human imagination. They are not merely collections of trees but the embodiment of life, inspiration, and profound connections to our planet. As we stand at the crossroads of environmental challenges and opportunities, the conservation and sustainable management of our forests have become paramount to securing a vibrant and harmonious future.

In the heart of Nigeria, where lush landscapes and vibrant communities converge, we find ourselves on a journey—one that explores the intricate dance between humanity and nature, progress and preservation. This book, "Sustaining Our Forests," is a testament to our unwavering commitment to this journey.

In the pages that follow, we embark on a voyage into the captivating world of sustainable forestry in Nigeria. Our aim is not merely to impart knowledge but to kindle a shared passion for safeguarding our forests. We believe that by illuminating the intricate tapestry of Nigeria's forests, from the verdant expanses to the intricate ecosystems they harbor, we can inspire a collective resolve to protect and nurture these vital resources.

Our exploration takes us to the Forestry Research Institute of Nigeria, a beacon of scientific inquiry and innovation dedicated to unraveling the mysteries of our forests and charting a path towards their sustainable stewardship. Within these hallowed halls, researchers and conservationists work tirelessly to harness the power of knowledge, to apply scientific principles, and to champion practices that resonate with the rhythms of nature.

We delve into the past, drawing lessons from historical examples of unsustainable forestry practices. We confront the harsh realities of deforestation, an issue that has left indelible scars on our landscapes. But we also find hope in the form of adaptation, exemplified by Anambra

State's visionary reforestation initiative, which serves as a shining testament to the transformative potential of collective action.

As we traverse through the chapters, we underscore the fundamental truth that our forests are not just a resource; they are the guardians of our planet's health, the custodians of biodiversity, and the custodians of countless lives and livelihoods. Sustainable forestry practices offer a path toward balance, ensuring that the legacy we leave for future generations is one of abundance, not scarcity.

The journey we undertake in this book is not one we travel alone. It is an invitation, extended to every reader, to become a guardian of the green, a protector of the forests. Whether you are an environmental enthusiast, a policymaker, a community leader, or simply someone who cherishes the beauty of nature, your role in this endeavor is pivotal.

As we embark on this odyssey into the heart of Nigeria's forests, we do so with a profound sense of responsibility and hope. May this book serve as a beacon of knowledge and inspiration, illuminating the path toward a future where our forests flourish, our ecosystems thrive, and our communities prosper.

Together, we can nurture Nigeria's forests for future generations and secure a legacy that will endure through the ages.

With gratitude and a shared commitment to our forests,

**Evaristus Chukwugoziem Okonkwo**
Nnewi, Anambra State
Nigeria

CHAPTER 1

## Introduction

Forests are not merely vast stretches of trees; they are the lungs of our planet, the keepers of biodiversity, and the providers of a multitude of resources upon which our societies depend. Throughout human history, forests have been central to our survival, offering sustenance, shelter, and inspiration. Yet, their preservation and responsible management are more critical today than ever before. In this opening chapter, we embark on a journey that explores the vital importance of sustainable forestry, delves into the consequences of historical unsustainable practices, and underscores the urgent need for adaptation in Nigeria, with a particular focus on the enchanting landscape of Anambra State.

## The Importance of Sustainable Forestry

Sustainable forestry represents a commitment to stewardship—a pledge to manage our forests in a manner that ensures they endure for generations to come. It recognizes that forests are not merely a resource to exploit, but a delicate and intricate ecosystem deserving of careful tending. At its core, sustainable forestry seeks to strike a harmonious balance between human needs and the preservation of these majestic habitats.

Forests serve as reservoirs of life, harboring countless species of plants and animals. They act as carbon sinks, capturing and storing carbon dioxide, a pivotal factor in mitigating climate change. They provide clean water, enhance air quality, and offer a myriad of medicinal and food resources. Moreover, forests are an essential component of the cultural and spiritual fabric of many societies, embodying a profound connection to the land.

## Advancing Sustainable Forestry in Nigeria: A Commitment to Conservation.

Safeguarding Nigeria's rich forest resources demands a resolute commitment to sustainable forestry practices. At the forefront of this mission stands the Forestry Research Institute of Nigeria, a bastion of scientific inquiry and innovation dedicated to orchestrating the prudent management and preservation of our forests—a legacy befitting the needs of both current and future generations. Their extensive research portfolio encompasses a diverse array of crucial subjects, ranging from sustainable forest management methodologies to the preservation of biodiversity, the mitigation of climate change impacts, and the exploration of the profound socio-economic benefits rooted within Nigeria's forests.

### The Imperative of Sustainable Forestry Practices

A crucial understanding underpins the imperative for sustainable forestry practices: the inextricable link between our well-being and the health of our forests. Historically, Nigeria, like many other nations, has grappled with unsustainable forestry practices that have, in turn, propelled deforestation. This alarming trend threatened not only the forests themselves but the entire ecological equilibrium that depends on their vitality.

In recognition of the gravity of this challenge, the Nigerian government has taken a definitive step forward. The launch of a National Forest Policy stands as a resounding declaration of intent—a pledge to harness the country's forest resources sustainably, acknowledging their irreplaceable value to our nation's environment, economy, and heritage.

### The Need for Adaptation: Anambra State's Reforestation Initiative

Adaptation serves as the cornerstone of our commitment to sustainable forestry practices in Nigeria. A case in point is the proactive stance of Anambra State, where the government has embarked on a visionary reforestation program. This program is a robust response to the ongoing threat of deforestation, as it seeks to rejuvenate and expand the state's forest cover. It serves as a beacon of hope—a testament to the transformative potential of deliberate, forward-thinking policies and actions in the face of environmental challenges.

As we embark on a journey through the pages of this narrative, we delve deeper into the realm of sustainable forestry in Nigeria. Together, we shall explore innovative approaches, lessons learned from the past, and the unwavering commitment of both institutions and individuals to secure a sustainable and thriving future for our forests. In the following chapters, we will uncover the multifaceted facets of forest conservation, delve into the intricacies of policy implementation, and witness the transformative power of collective action, exemplified by Anambra State's inspiring reforestation endeavors.

This book therefore, explores how sustainable forestry is not a mere aspiration but an achievable reality that promises a future where forests thrive, ecosystems flourish, and communities prosper. It underscores the intertwined relationship between environmental, economic, and social dimensions, highlighting the need for holistic solutions.

**Historical Examples of Unsustainable Practices**

As we embark on our journey into the world of sustainable forestry, it is essential to heed the lessons of history. Across the annals of time, there are poignant examples of societies that, unwittingly or not, exploited their forests to the brink of devastation. One such cautionary tale is that of the Indus Valley people, some 3,500 years ago.

In their quest to build magnificent cities, they made the fateful decision to fell forests across hundreds of miles to fire the bricks needed for construction. The consequence of their actions was catastrophic; when the rains ceased, all 1,000 of their cities were abandoned. This sobering example underscores the peril of disregarding the ecological foundations of our societies and the importance of learning from our predecessors' mistakes.

**The Need for Adaptation in Nigeria, with a Focus on Anambra State.**

Now, we turn our gaze to the rich and diverse landscapes of Nigeria, with a particular focus on the enchanting Anambra State. Nigeria is a nation blessed with abundant natural resources, and its forests play a pivotal role in maintaining ecological balance, supporting livelihoods, and contributing to its cultural tapestry. However, rapid urbanization, deforestation, agricultural expansion, and illegal logging pose imminent threats to these precious ecosystems.

Anambra State, nestled in South East, Nigeria, is graced with a unique blend of lush forests, fertile farmlands, and vibrant communities. Yet, it is not immune to the challenges that confront the nation's forests. This chapter serves as a clarion call for adaptation—a call to recognize the pressing need to protect and sustainably manage Anambra's forests.

In the chapters that follow, we will explore the multifaceted dimensions of sustainable forestry, unveil strategies for responsible forest management, and present a vision of a greener future where Anambra State's forests stand as a testament to our commitment to environmental and economic harmony. Together, we embark on a journey to safeguard the natural treasures of this land for generations yet unborn.

CHAPTER 2

## Understanding Sustainable Forestry

Forests, often called the lungs of our planet, have sustained life for millennia. However, the continued well-being of these vital ecosystems now depends on our ability to practice sustainable forestry. In this chapter, we embark on a journey to understand the multifaceted dimensions of sustainable forestry, from its definition to the intricate interplay of environmental, economic, and social factors. We also examine the global and regional challenges that shape the practice of sustainable forestry.

## Defining Sustainable Forestry

Sustainable forestry is a term often used, but its essence lies in its interpretation and application. At its core, sustainable forestry represents a commitment to manage forests in a way that ensures their continued health and productivity over the long term. It is a harmonious coexistence between human needs and the preservation of the ecological and cultural values that forests offer.

## Sustainable Forestry: Balancing Present and Future Needs

Sustainable forestry embodies the art of nurturing and managing forests in a manner that not only caters to the demands of the present generation but, more crucially, safeguards the capacity of future generations to fulfill their own needs. It is a delicate and intricate dance that harmonizes the requirements of the environment, the well-being of wildlife, and the prosperity of forest communities, all while conserving the invaluable legacy of our forests for the tomorrows that await.

## Three Dimensions of Sustainability

Sustainable forestry seeks to balance three fundamental pillars: Environmental, Economic, and Social Dimensions.

1. Environmental Sustainability: This pillar focuses on maintaining the health and vitality of forest ecosystems. It involves practices that minimize harm to soil, water, and wildlife, while also promoting biodiversity conservation and carbon sequestration. Environmental Dimension of Sustainable forestry practices prioritize the health and resilience of forest ecosystems. This includes maintaining habitat diversity, safeguarding water quality, and addressing threats like invasive species and wildfire. This dimension revolves around the well-being and diversity of forest ecosystems. It encompasses practices aimed at preserving the vitality of forests, safeguarding their ecological balance, and protecting the myriad species that call these ecosystems home. In essence, it seeks to ensure that forests continue to thrive as thriving ecosystems.

2. Economic Dimension: Economic viability is crucial for sustainable forestry. It entails using forests to generate income and livelihoods without depleting them to a point where their capacity to regenerate is compromised. Economic sustainability is achieved by optimizing the use of forest resources while ensuring the long-term viability of forest-based industries. This involves careful planning, including reforestation and sustainable harvest levels. The economic dimension of sustainable forestry is an intricate endeavor that revolves around the responsible utilization of forest resources. It is not merely about extracting timber or forest products; it's about doing so efficiently and effectively. Sustainable forestry endeavors to support livelihoods and economies while ensuring that this utilization does not compromise the ability of forests to regenerate and flourish.

3. Social Dimension: Communities that depend on forests for their well-being and way of life must benefit from forestry activities. Social

sustainability includes considerations like local employment, community engagement, and the recognition of indigenous rights and knowledge. Forests are often intricately tied to the livelihoods and cultures of local communities, including indigenous groups. Sustainable forestry recognizes these relationships and strives to empower and benefit these communities while respecting their traditions and knowledge. It is a bedrock principle of sustainable forestry. It revolves around the equitable management of forests, considering the rights and well-being of local communities, including indigenous groups. It also emphasizes community engagement, ensuring that those who live in proximity to forests have a meaningful say in how these vital resources are managed.

Sustainable forestry is therefore a dynamic concept that balances these three dimensions. At its heart, sustainable forestry is a trifold concept, manifesting in three distinct dimensions, each as vital as the other.

**Global ,Regional and Local Hurdles to Sustainability**

As we journey deeper into the world of sustainable forestry, we must confront and surmount various global and regional challenges:

**Global and Regional Challenges**

Sustainable forestry is not without its challenges, both on a global and regional scale:

1. Global Challenges: On a global level, challenges such as climate change, illegal logging, and the international trade in forest products demand collaborative solutions. Initiatives like forest certification programs (e.g., FSC and PEFC) aim to address these issues and promote sustainable forestry practices worldwide. These encompass formidable issues that transcend borders and demand global cooperation. Climate change casts a long shadow, impacting forest health and biodiversity. Deforestation, driven by agriculture and infrastructure development, threatens forests worldwide. Illegal logging, with its devastating environmental and economic consequences, poses a significant hurdle, as does the creeping specter of forest degradation.

2. Regional Challenges: The challenges faced by different regions are as diverse as the landscapes they encompass. The challenges faced by regions can vary widely based on factors like climate, forest type, and population density. In some regions, deforestation for agriculture or infrastructure development is a significant concern, while in others, the risk may be unsustainable logging or loss of biodiversity.

Land-use change, driven by agricultural expansion or urbanization, can lead to significant deforestation in some areas. Population growth can exert immense pressure on forest resources. Poverty can drive unsustainable resource extraction. Each region faces its unique blend of challenges, necessitating localized solutions and strategies.

3. Local Challenges in Anambra State: Sustainable forests, which aim to fulfill the diverse needs of present and future generations across social, economic, ecological, cultural, and spiritual realms, offer a multitude of benefits including biodiversity preservation, climate regulation, soil protection, water purification, timber production, recreation, and cultural significance. However, in Anambra State, located in southeastern Nigeria with a population of approximately 5.5 million people, sustainable forests confront several pressing challenges.

1. Loss of Forest Reserves: A study conducted by Onyeizugbe et al. (2021) reveals that forest reserves in Anambra State are diminishing at a rate of 3.5% annually due to factors like encroachment, excisions, and outright de-reservations. The Apakah Forest Reserve in Onitsha North Local Government Area serves as a case in point, having lost around 90% of its original area since 1976. This loss has detrimental environmental consequences such as erosion, flooding, altered local climate conditions, siltation of water bodies, and the extinction of plant and animal species.

2. Weak Governance and Policy Implementation: Another obstacle to sustainable forests in Anambra State is the ineffective governance and inadequate policy enforcement. The Forest Policy Act of 2006 remains largely unimplemented at both state and local government levels, existing merely on paper. Contributing factors include corruption, ignorance, insecurity, population growth, urban expansion, and excessive consumption. Stakeholders have called for increased collaboration among

communities and individuals to combat deforestation and forest degradation in Anambra State and Nigeria as a whole.

3. Low Awareness and Participation: A third challenge is the low level of awareness and engagement among the populace. Many individuals are unaware of the value and significance of forests for their livelihoods and overall well-being. Furthermore, they do not actively participate in forest management activities such as tree planting, protection, and monitoring. Addressing this trend requires widespread sensitization and awareness campaigns on natural resource management, as well as influencing policy direction in forest management.

To tackle these challenges, several potential solutions emerge:

1. Developing a Sustainable Forest Management Model: Onyeizugbe et al. (2021) have proposed a model for sustainable forest management in Anambra State. This model emphasizes community involvement, awareness creation, effective policy implementation, staff training, and categorization of forest reserve loss into three phases: input, throughput, and output.

2. Enforcing Laws and Regulations: Enforcing laws and regulations that safeguard forests against illegal activities such as logging, mining, farming, and encroachment is crucial. Strict penalties for offenders and incentives for compliance, along with transparent and accountable allocation and management of forest resources, can help protect these vital ecosystems.

3. Promoting Alternative Livelihoods: Providing alternative livelihood options for those dependent on forests for income is essential. This may involve facilitating access to credit, markets, education, healthcare, and other social services. Supporting initiatives like agroforestry, ecotourism, non-timber forest products, and other forest-compatible income-generating activities can mitigate the pressure on forests for sustenance.

4. "Inadequate forest guards" is indeed another significant driver contributing to the challenges faced by sustainable forests in Anambra

State. The shortage of forest guards in the region exacerbates the existing problems and poses additional threats to the health and preservation of the state's forests.

**Need to employ more forest guards**

Let's discuss why there is a compelling need to employ more forest guards not just in Anambra State but across the federation:

1. Illegal Activities and Poaching: An insufficient number of forest guards means there are not enough personnel to patrol and protect the forests adequately. This creates opportunities for illegal activities such as illegal logging, hunting, and poaching to thrive. Without a sufficient presence of forest guards, it becomes difficult to detect and deter these harmful practices.

2. Encroachment and Land Conversion: Forests often face encroachment from agricultural and urban expansion. More forest guards are needed to monitor and prevent these encroachments, ensuring that forested areas are not converted into farmlands or urban developments. This is crucial for preserving the ecological balance and the various ecosystem services that forests provide.

3. Fire Prevention and Management: Forest fires can have devastating effects on forest ecosystems. Forest guards play a crucial role in preventing and managing forest fires. They can monitor for early signs of fires, educate the local population on fire prevention, and coordinate firefighting efforts. Insufficient staffing can lead to delayed responses and greater damage during forest fires.

4. Illegal Logging and Timber Trade: Anambra State, like many regions, may suffer from illegal logging activities. Forest guards are essential in monitoring and regulating timber harvesting activities to ensure they comply with sustainable practices and legal requirements. Insufficient staffing can result in a lack of oversight and enforcement of logging regulations.

5. Wildlife Protection: Protecting the diverse wildlife within the forests is essential for biodiversity conservation. Forest guards play a critical role in

safeguarding these species from poaching and habitat destruction. Without an adequate presence of guards, wildlife populations can be threatened, potentially leading to species endangerment or extinction.

6. Community Engagement: Forest guards often work closely with local communities, educating them about sustainable forest management and involving them in conservation efforts. With more forest guards, there can be increased engagement and collaboration with these communities, fostering a sense of shared responsibility for forest conservation.

7. Data Collection and Monitoring: Forest guards are instrumental in collecting data on the state of the forests, including changes in biodiversity, vegetation health, and ecosystem dynamics. This information is essential for making informed decisions about forest management and conservation strategies.

In summary, employing more forest guards in Anambra State is imperative to address the numerous challenges faced by sustainable forests. These guards serve as the frontline defenders of forests, helping to combat illegal activities, preserve biodiversity, prevent forest fires, and engage with local communities. Adequate staffing not only protects the environment but also contributes to the long-term social and economic well-being of the region. Therefore, increasing the number of forest guards should be considered a vital step in promoting sustainable forest management and conservation in Anambra State.

As we delve deeper into each dimension and challenge of sustainable forestry, we embark on a journey that explores the intricate interplay between environmental stewardship, economic viability, and social equity. Together, we aim to forge a path toward a world where our forests thrive, and the needs of both present and future generations find harmonious balance amid the splendor of nature.

Conclusion: In this chapter, we have taken our initial steps towards comprehending the concept of sustainable forestry—a holistic approach that acknowledges the interconnectedness of the environment, the economy, and society. As we progress on this journey, we will delve further into each dimension, examining practical strategies, global success stories, and the pivotal role that sustainable forestry plays in securing a more equitable and prosperous future for our forests and humanity.

CHAPTER 3

## The Ecological Imperatives

Within the towering canopies and hushed undergrowth of forests, a symphony of life unfolds—a symphony that resonates not only with the present but also echoes through the corridors of the future. In this chapter, we embark on a journey to unearth the profound ecological imperatives that cast forests as the bedrock of ecological vitality. We navigate through the intricate web of forest ecosystems, explore their pivotal role in biodiversity conservation, and decipher their fundamental contribution to carbon sequestration and climate change mitigation.

## The Guardians of Ecosystem Health

Forests are the guardians of ecosystem health, serving as the architects of balance and biodiversity. They house an astounding array of life, from the towering giants that reach for the skies to the microscopic organisms that teem in the forest floor's shadows. Birds, mammals, insects, fungi, and plants all play their unique roles in the intricate dance of forest ecosystems.

Forests play a pivotal role in moderating local climates, influencing temperature, humidity, and rainfall patterns. Acting as nature's sponges, they absorb rainfall and gradually release it, mitigating the threat of both floods and droughts. Moreover, forests act as natural filters, enhancing air and water quality by trapping pollutants and providing a source of pristine water for communities downstream.

## Preservation of Biodiversity: Forests as Sanctuaries of Life

Forests are akin to grand treasure troves of biodiversity, housing a mesmerizing array of species, many of which remain undiscovered and unnamed. From the iridescent plumage of tropical birds to the enigmatic movements of large mammals, forests resonate with the vibrant symphony of life.

Biodiversity conservation lies at the heart of the forest imperative. It entails the preservation of diverse species and the protection of their habitats. Forests, as sanctuaries to rare and endemic species, play a pivotal role in the global effort to conserve biodiversity. Their loss not only extinguishes unique life forms but also disrupts the delicate ecological interactions that underpin life on Earth.

## Carbon Sequestration and the Battle against Climate Change

In the quiet realm of forests, an unheralded battle unfolds—one against the urgent threat of climate change. Through a process known as carbon sequestration, forests quietly absorb carbon dioxide from the atmosphere, storing it as organic matter. This process acts as a crucial brake on the surging concentrations of greenhouse gases that drive global warming.

Carbon sequestration is the process of capturing and storing carbon dioxide ($CO_2$) from the atmosphere or from human activities, such as burning fossil fuels and industrial livestock production, to prevent or delay global warming and climate change. Carbon sequestration can be done in different ways, such as:

Biological sequestration: This involves using plants, algae, and microorganisms to capture and store $CO_2$ through photosynthesis. Examples of biological sequestration include afforestation, reforestation, agroforestry, bio char, ocean fertilization, and enhanced weathering.

Geological sequestration: This involves injecting $CO_2$ into underground geological formations, such as depleted oil and gas reservoirs, saline aquifers, or coal seams. Examples of geological sequestration include carbon capture and storage (CCS), enhanced oil recovery (EOR), and enhanced coal bed methane (ECBM).

Chemical sequestration: This involves converting $CO_2$ into stable compounds, such as carbonates, bicarbonates, or polymers. Examples of chemical sequestration include mineral carbonation, electrochemical reduction, and polymerization.

Carbon sequestration can help us fight against climate change by reducing the concentration of $CO_2$ in the atmosphere and the ocean, which are the main drivers of the greenhouse effect and ocean acidification. According to the Intergovernmental Panel on Climate Change (IPCC), carbon sequestration can contribute to limiting global warming to 1.5°C or 2°C above pre-industrial levels by 2100. However, carbon sequestration also faces many challenges, such as:

Technical challenges: Carbon sequestration requires advanced technologies that are still under development or not widely deployed. For example, CCS is expensive, energy-intensive, and not commercially viable in many sectors. Biological sequestration is limited by land availability, water scarcity, and nutrient cycling. Chemical sequestration is often slow, costly, and environmentally harmful.

Environmental challenges: Carbon sequestration can have negative impacts on the environment, such as biodiversity loss, soil degradation, water pollution, leakage risks, and public health hazards. For example, afforestation can reduce native species diversity and alter ecosystem services. Ocean fertilization can cause harmful algal blooms and oxygen depletion. Mineral carbonation can generate large amounts of waste and consume natural resources.

Social challenges: Carbon sequestration can face social barriers, such as public acceptance, ethical concerns, legal frameworks, and governance issues. For example, CCS can raise questions about liability, ownership, and regulation of CO2 storage sites. Agroforestry can affect food security and land tenure rights. Ocean fertilization can violate international conventions and agreements.

Therefore, carbon sequestration is not a silver bullet solution to climate change. It needs to be combined with other mitigation strategies, such as reducing greenhouse gas emissions, increasing energy efficiency, and switching to renewable energy sources. It also needs to be supported by scientific research, policy incentives, stakeholder engagement, and public education.

Forests, particularly ancient and tropical forests, are repositories of carbon. Their preservation and rejuvenation are essential in the global struggle against climate change. By curtailing carbon emissions and amplifying carbon storage, forests emerge as nature's champions in the fight against climate change.

Additionally, forests are instrumental in creating what is often termed the "forest effect." They sculpt local and regional climates, tempering extreme temperatures and shaping precipitation patterns. In so doing, they aid communities in adapting to the evolving climate landscape, reducing the vulnerability to climate-related disasters.

In this chapter, we have embarked on a voyage to uncover the ecological imperatives that render forests as the linchpins of ecological well-being. They are not mere collections of trees but the guardians of life, the sentinels of pure air and water, and the staunch defenders against climate change. As our journey progresses, we will venture deeper into the intricate relationships between forests and biodiversity, unveiling the critical role they play in our collective endeavor to combat climate change.

CHAPTER 4

## The Economics of Forests

Forests are far more than just nature's grandeur; they are also integral threads in the economic fabric of societies worldwide. In this chapter, we navigate the intricate landscape of economic considerations surrounding forests. We explore the invaluable contributions of forests to local economies, the delicate equilibrium between economic interests and conservation imperatives, and the potential of sustainable forest management as a transformative economic strategy.

## The Valuable Role of Forests in Local Economies

Forests are dynamic economic engines that drive local prosperity. They provide a diverse array of resources that sustain livelihoods, foster industries, and generate revenue streams for communities worldwide.

Timber and Non-Timber Forest Products (NTFPs): Timber, when harvested sustainably, serves as a fundamental building block for construction and furniture industries. Equally vital are NTFPs, ranging from fruits, nuts, and mushrooms to medicinal plants and resins. These products not only provide sustenance but also opportunities for income generation.

Employment and Income: Forests offer a broad spectrum of employment opportunities, from the forest floor to processing mills and beyond. Communities dependent on forests often find economic stability through jobs in logging, forest management, and the manufacture of forest products.

Tourism and Recreation: Forests beckon tourists and nature enthusiasts, significantly contributing to local economies. Activities like hiking, wildlife watching, and eco-tourism attract visitors, bolstering local businesses and services.

## Balancing Economic Interests with Conservation

Harmonizing economic interests with conservation is a complex art, one that necessitates responsible and sustainable practices. While forests provide economic opportunities, unchecked exploitation can exact a toll on the very resources sustaining local economies.

Overharvesting timber, illegal logging, and unchecked deforestation can deplete forests beyond their capacity to regenerate. This not only jeopardizes the environment but also threatens the long-term economic viability of forest-dependent communities.

## Sustainable Forest Management as an Economic Strategy

Sustainable forest management (SFM) is the practice of managing forests in a way that meets the needs of the present without compromising the ability of future generations to meet their own needs. Sustainable forest management emerges as a beacon of hope in the quest for both economic prosperity and ecological responsibility. It strives to maximize the benefits of forests while ensuring their continued health and vitality.

## Key tenets of sustainable forest management encompass:

- Balancing Harvest and Regeneration: Sustainable forestry practices maintain a delicate equilibrium, ensuring that the rate of harvesting aligns with the rate of forest regeneration. This guarantees a perpetual supply of forest resources.

- Preserving Ecosystem Health: Sustainable forest management prioritizes the preservation of forest ecosystems, safeguarding biodiversity and ecosystem services.

- Community Engagement: It actively engages local communities in decision-making, respecting their rights and recognizing their role as stewards of the land.

- Certification and Best Practices: Many sustainable forestry initiatives benefit from certification programs, such as the Forest Stewardship Council (FSC) and the Programme for the Endorsement of Forest

Certification (PEFC). These programs promote responsible forest management practices.

- Value Addition: Sustainable forest management encourages the development of value-added forest products and local processing, enhancing economic returns within communities.

SFM aims to balance the environmental, social, and economic aspects of forests, such as biodiversity, livelihoods, and timber production[1]. SFM is relevant to Nigeria and Africa because:

- Forests are important for the continent's development and well-being: Africa has about 624 million hectares of forests, which cover 20.6% of its land area and represent 15.6% of the world's forest cover. African forests provide a range of goods and services that support the livelihoods of millions of people, such as food, fuel, medicine, materials, income, and employment. African forests also contribute to the global climate regulation by sequestering about 7.6 gigatonnes of carbon dioxide per year, equivalent to 15% of global emissions.

- Forests are under threat from various drivers of deforestation and degradation: Africa loses about 3.9 million hectares of forest per year, which is the second highest rate in the world after South America. The main drivers of deforestation and degradation in Africa include agricultural expansion, logging, mining, infrastructure development, urbanization, population growth, poverty, and conflicts. These drivers reduce the forest area, quality, and diversity, and undermine the benefits that forests provide to people and nature.

- Forests are part of the solution to address the challenges facing the continent: SFM can help Africa achieve its development goals and aspirations, such as the Agenda 2063, the Sustainable Development Goals, and the Paris Agreement. SFM can enhance the resilience of forests and people to climate change, disasters, and diseases. SFM can also promote the transition to a green economy by creating opportunities for sustainable production and consumption of forest products and services. SFM can also foster peace and security by reducing conflicts over forest resources and enhancing cooperation among stakeholders.

Therefore, SFM is a vital strategy for Nigeria and Africa to conserve and restore their forests while ensuring their contribution to the continent's prosperity and stability.

SFM can also contribute to the achievement of the Sustainable Development Goals (SDGs), the Paris Agreement, and the European Green Deal by:

Reducing greenhouse gas emissions and enhancing carbon sinks: Forests play a key role in mitigating climate change by absorbing and storing carbon dioxide (CO2) from the atmosphere. According to the Global Forest Goals Report 2021, forests sequestered about 7.6 gigatonnes of CO2 per year from 2011 to 2015, equivalent to 15% of global CO2 emissions. SFM can help maintain and increase the carbon storage capacity of forests by preventing deforestation, degradation, and disturbances, and by promoting afforestation, restoration, and adaptation.

Supporting the bioeconomy and circular economy: Forests provide a renewable source of biomass that can be used for various purposes, such as energy, materials, chemicals, and bioproducts. The forest-based sector plays a crucial role in the bioeconomy, encompassing the utilization of biological resources, processes, and principles to deliver goods and services across all economic sectors[1]. In the context of Africa, and specifically Nigeria, this sector holds profound importance by:

1. Economic Vitality and Job Creation: According to a comprehensive report from the United Nations Economic Commission for Africa (UNECA), the forest-based sector contributes significantly to Africa's gross domestic product (GDP), accounting for approximately 6% of the continent's GDP. Moreover, it provides livelihoods for approximately 12.5 million individuals, primarily within the informal sector. In Nigeria, this sector contributes around 3.5% of the nation's GDP and offers employment opportunities to roughly 4.5 million people, predominantly in rural areas.

2. Provision of Diverse Goods and Services: The forest-based sector serves as a wellspring of diverse goods and services, contributing to human well-being and societal advancement. These encompass a wide

spectrum of offerings, including timber, fuelwood, non-timber forest products (NTFPs), ecosystem services, and cultural values. For instance, NTFPs such as fruits, nuts, honey, medicinal plants, and bushmeat constitute vital sources of sustenance, nutrition, health, and income for millions of Africans. Ecosystem services, including carbon sequestration, water regulation, soil preservation, and biodiversity conservation, play a pivotal role in climate change mitigation and adaptation.

3. Driving Innovation and Sustainability: The forest-based sector is a catalyst for innovation and sustainability through the development of novel products and processes grounded in renewable biomass and circular economy principles. Biorefineries, for instance, can convert forest biomass into biofuels, bioplastics, biopharmaceuticals, and other bioproducts that offer sustainable alternatives to fossil-based materials and mitigate greenhouse gas emissions. Sustainable forest management practices enhance the resilience and productivity of forests, reducing vulnerability to threats such as deforestation, degradation, fires, pests, and diseases.

In conclusion, the forest-based sector stands as a substantial contributor to the broader bioeconomy in Africa and, more specifically, Nigeria. Its multifaceted contributions align with the developmental objectives and aspirations of the continent, including Agenda 2063, the Sustainable Development Goals, and the Paris Agreement. Consequently, recognizing and harnessing the potential of the forest-based sector can substantially bolster economic growth, employment, innovation, and sustainability across Africa.

SFM can help ensure the sustainable production and use of forest biomass by applying the cascading principle, increasing resource efficiency, reducing waste, and fostering innovation.

Forests also host more than 80% of the world's terrestrial biodiversity and are home to many endangered species. SFM can help preserve and enhance the ecosystem services and biodiversity of forests by maintaining their structure, function, and diversity, and by restoring degraded forests.

Providing ecosystem services and biodiversity conservation: Forests offer a range of benefits that support human well-being and the environment, such as water regulation, soil protection, air quality improvement, pollination, recreation, and cultural heritage.

## To implement SFM as an economic strategy, some possible actions are:

Developing a common definition and criteria for SFM: There is currently no agreed definition or criteria for SFM at the AU level. This creates confusion and inconsistency among different policies and stakeholders. A common AU definition and criteria for SFM would provide a clear and coherent framework for forest management across the AU and facilitate monitoring and reporting.

Strengthening forest governance and stakeholder participation: Forest governance refers to the rules, institutions, processes, and practices that shape how forests are managed. Stakeholder participation refers to the involvement of all relevant actors in forest decision-making, such as forest owners, managers, users, communities, civil society, industry, academia, and public authorities. Effective forest governance and stakeholder participation are essential for ensuring the legitimacy, transparency, accountability, and inclusiveness of SFM.

## Increasing investments and incentives for SFM:

SFM requires adequate financial resources and incentives to cover the costs of forest management activities and to reward the provision of public goods and services. However, many forest owners and managers face difficulties in accessing funding sources or markets for their products or services. Therefore, there is a need to increase investments and incentives for SFM from various sources, such as public funds, private funds, payments for ecosystem services (PES), green bonds, carbon credits, or certification schemes

In this chapter, we've unraveled the intricate economic facets of forests. They are not mere resource banks but the lifeblood of countless livelihoods. As we continue our journey, we will delve deeper into the practical strategies and global success stories that underscore the transformative potential of sustainable forest management, bridging the realms of economics and ecology.

CHAPTER 5

## Social and Cultural Aspects

In the heart of sustainable forestry practices lie intricate layers of social and cultural dimensions, each as profound as the forests themselves. In this chapter, we delve into the vital interplay between indigenous knowledge and forest management, the pivotal role of local communities, and the invaluable lessons drawn from global forest stewardship models.

## Indigenous Knowledge and Forest Management

Indigenous knowledge is an invaluable treasure trove, enriched over generations by those who have cultivated a deep and intimate connection with forests. Indigenous peoples have developed sophisticated knowledge systems that encompass the intricate dance of forest ecosystems and the art of sustainable management.

Indigenous knowledge, a repository of local and traditional wisdom passed down through generations within a community or culture, shares an intimate connection with forest management in Nigeria. In this intricate relationship, many Nigerian communities draw upon forests for their sustenance, cultural richness, and identity. The synergy between indigenous knowledge and forest management in Nigeria can be observed through various interconnected avenues:

1. Guiding Sustainable Resource Use and Conservation: Nigerian communities have cultivated indigenous knowledge systems that offer guidance on the sustainable and efficient utilization of forest resources. This encompasses a deep understanding of the medicinal, nutritional, and economic worth of diverse plant and animal species, along with methods to harvest them without depleting these invaluable resources.

Additionally, they possess insights into the ecological cycles, seasons, and indicators influencing forest conditions and productivity. These insights inform the regulation of access and resource use according to customary laws, norms, and practices.

2. Supporting Forest Restoration and Adaptation: Indigenous knowledge systems in Nigeria extend to the restoration and adaptation of forests amidst evolving environmental and social dynamics. Communities have acquired knowledge related to the propagation, cultivation, and management of native tree species, enhancing their growth and resilience. Furthermore, they possess insights into the effects of climate change, disasters, and diseases on forests, alongside traditional coping mechanisms like fire management, pest control, and diversification. This knowledge is harnessed to rehabilitate degraded forests and bolster their resilience.

3. Reflecting Values and Beliefs: Indigenous knowledge systems in Nigeria mirror the values and beliefs of forest communities, encompassing spiritual, cultural, and historical significance. This wisdom underscores the importance of respecting and protecting forests. Additionally, it delineates the roles and responsibilities of various community members in forest management, including elders, leaders, women, youth, and children. This knowledge fosters social cohesion, participation, and empowerment within forest management initiatives.

Hence, indigenous knowledge and forest management in Nigeria are deeply intertwined and interdependent. Indigenous knowledge enriches forest management by incorporating local perspectives, experiences, and innovations, thereby improving outcomes. Simultaneously, forest management plays a pivotal role in preserving indigenous knowledge by recognizing its intrinsic value, relevance, and legitimacy within the context of sustainable forest conservation and utilization. This harmonious relationship represents a vital synergy that can contribute to the holistic well-being of both the forest ecosystems and the communities that depend on them.

Their wisdom extends from the identification of plant species with medicinal properties to the recognition of natural indicators of ecological health. Indigenous practices often revolve around non-destructive resource use, mindful of the delicate balance that sustains forests. These insights are a priceless resource for informing sustainable forest management practices.

By integrating indigenous knowledge into forestry strategies, we unlock the potential for not only conserving forests but also preserving and respecting the cultures and traditions of indigenous communities. It offers a pathway to harmonious coexistence between humanity and nature.

## The Role of Local Communities

Local communities harbor a profound relationship with forests, stemming from dependence on these ecosystems for their livelihoods and cultural identities. Their stewardship is often guided by traditions that have evolved over centuries, fostering a deep-rooted respect for the land.

Sustainable forest management practices must recognize the significance of local communities. Engagement and collaboration with these communities are paramount, considering their unique insights and needs. Equitable decision-making, respect for customary rights, and shared benefits from forest resources are essential aspects of this partnership.

## Lessons from Global Forest Stewardship Models

Global forest stewardship models, exemplified by initiatives like the Forest Stewardship Council (FSC), offer valuable frameworks for sustainable forest management. These models provide guidelines, standards, and certification systems that promote responsible forestry practices on a global scale.

The FSC, for instance, emphasizes principles like biodiversity conservation, community engagement, and responsible harvesting. Lessons from such models offer inspiration and a blueprint for adapting sustainable forest management practices to local contexts.

These models underscore the significance of certification and third-party verification in ensuring adherence to sustainable practices, building trust with consumers, and enhancing market access for responsibly sourced forest products.


In this chapter, we've unveiled the intricate web of social and cultural aspects that intertwine with sustainable forestry practices. Indigenous knowledge offers a profound reservoir of wisdom, local communities serve as guardians of the land, and global forest stewardship models illuminate the path toward responsible management. As we continue our exploration, we will unearth case studies and real-world examples that exemplify the integration of these dimensions into sustainable forestry, ensuring that our forests thrive for generations to come.

CHAPTER 6

## Lessons from Global Models

In the tapestry of sustainable forestry practices, global models and international agreements cast a guiding light, illuminating pathways towards responsible forest management. In this chapter, we explore case studies of successful sustainable forestry practices, the profound impact of international agreements like FSC certification, and the vital process of adapting global models to the unique context of Nigeria.

## Case Studies of Successful Sustainable Forestry Practices

Around the world, there exist shining examples of sustainable forestry practices that stand as beacons of hope and inspiration. These case studies demonstrate that it is possible to balance economic interests, ecological imperatives, and societal needs.

One notable reference is the Global Forest Goals Report 2021, which offers a comprehensive evaluation of the world's progress in implementing the United Nations Strategic Plan for Forests 2030. This report provides a snapshot of actions taken by countries and organizations, showcasing initiatives that contribute to achieving the six Global Forest Goals. These case studies offer valuable insights into how sustainable forestry practices can be effectively implemented at regional and national levels.

## The Impact of International Agreements: FSC Certification

The Forest Stewardship Council (FSC) stands as a powerful emblem of international collaboration in promoting responsible forest management.

This certification system provides a robust framework for forest management that balances environmental suitability, social benefits, and economic viability.

FSC certification offers a myriad of advantages. It assures consumers that forest products have been sourced responsibly and sustainably, driving market demand for such products. It also fosters greater transparency in supply chains, allowing businesses to demonstrate their commitment to responsible sourcing.

The impact of FSC certification extends beyond economic benefits. It bolsters the conservation of forest ecosystems, supports the rights of indigenous peoples and local communities, and encourages the adoption of best practices in forestry. Lessons from the success of FSC certification illuminate the transformative potential of international agreements in promoting sustainable forest management.

**Adaptation of Global Models to Nigeria**

Global models for sustainable forest management (SFM) are frameworks or guidelines that aim to promote the conservation and enhancement of forest resources and their benefits for present and future generations.

For Nigeria, the journey towards sustainable forestry practices is informed by both local realities and global wisdom. The Nigerian government has taken a significant step by launching a National Forest Policy, heralding a commitment to the sustainable utilization of the country's forest resources.

Some examples of global models for SFM are:

- The United Nations Strategic Plan for Forests 2017-2030, which provides a global vision, mission, objectives, and targets for forests and a reference framework for national action and international cooperation.

- The Sustainable Development Goals, which include several targets related to forests, such as 15.1 (ensure the conservation, restoration and sustainable use of terrestrial and inland freshwater ecosystems and their services), 15.2 (promote the implementation of sustainable management of all types of forests), and 15.b (mobilize significant resources from all sources and at all levels to finance sustainable forest management).

- The Forest Principles, which are a set of non-legally binding statements that provide a basis for the conservation and sustainable development of forests, such as respecting the rights and interests of forest-dependent people, integrating forest values into economic and social development, promoting scientific research and education on forests, and enhancing international cooperation on forest issues[4].

These global models can be adapted to Nigeria's forest in general and Anambra State's forest in particular by:

- Developing a national forest policy and legislation that are aligned with the global models and reflect the specific needs, challenges, and opportunities of Nigeria's forest sector.

- Implementing a national forest inventory and monitoring system that can provide reliable and up-to-date information on the status, trends, and changes of forest resources and their uses.

- Establishing a national forest fund that can mobilize financial resources from various sources, such as public funds, private funds, payments for ecosystem services, green bonds, carbon credits, or certification schemes, to support SFM activities.

- Enhancing the capacity and participation of stakeholders in SFM, such as federal, state, and local governments, forest owners and managers, communities, civil society, industry, academia, and international partners.

- Promoting the restoration and conservation of forest reserves in Anambra State, such as Ossomala Forest Reserve in Ogbaru Local Government Area, which has lost about 90% of its original area since 1976 due to encroachment, excisions, and outright de-reservations.

- Supporting the sustainable use and management of community forests in Anambra State, such as Ozubulu community forest in Ekwusigo Local

Government Area, which provides goods and services such as timber, fuelwood, non-timber forest products (NTFPs), ecosystem services, and cultural values to local users.

- Fostering innovation and sustainability in the forest-based sector in Anambra State by developing new products and processes that are based on renewable biomass and circular economy principles.

The adaptation of global models to Nigeria's context is a crucial endeavor. It involves aligning international best practices, such as those championed by FSC certification, with the unique ecological, economic, and social landscape of the nation. This process ensures that sustainable forest management strategies resonate with the aspirations and needs of local communities, fostering a harmonious coexistence between people and nature.

In this chapter, we have traversed the globe to glean insights from successful sustainable forestry practices, recognized the far-reaching impact of international agreements like FSC certification, and emphasized the importance of adapting global models to the specific contours of Nigeria's forest management journey. As our exploration continues, we will unearth further case studies and practical strategies that illuminate the path toward a sustainable and thriving forest ecosystem in Nigeria and beyond.

CHAPTER 7

## Nigeria's Forests and the Anambra State Context

Nigeria, often referred to as the "Giant of Africa," is a country of extraordinary diversity. Its landscapes range from the arid Sahel region in the north to the lush and verdant rainforests of the south. Nestled within this diverse tapestry are the nation's forests—natural treasures that contribute significantly to its ecological, economic, and cultural wealth. In this chapter, we embark on a journey to explore Nigeria's rich forest resources, delve into the unique challenges facing Anambra State, and unravel the intricate interplay between forests and water resources within the state.

## An Overview of Nigeria's Forest Resources

Nigeria's forests are a testament to the nation's ecological splendor. They are, in essence, living libraries of biodiversity, each with its unique stories to tell. These forests, which encompass a wide range of ecosystems, are vital for various reasons.

In the southern part of the country, where the climate is characterized by high rainfall and temperatures, one finds the tropical rainforests. These are among the world's most biologically diverse ecosystems, teeming with a profusion of flora and fauna. Here, towering hardwood trees, their canopies a verdant umbrella, shelter a mesmerizing array of life forms.

From the colorful plumage of tropical birds to the elusive movements of large mammals, Nigeria's rainforests are a symphony of biodiversity.

Moving northward, the landscape transforms into savannas and woodlands as rainfall becomes less abundant. These ecosystems support their own unique species and provide habitat for wildlife adapted to these conditions. Here, trees like the shea tree (Vitellaria paradoxa) and the African mahogany (Khaya senegalensis) play crucial roles in local economies.

Nigeria's forests are more than just a haven for biodiversity; they are also powerful contributors to the nation's economy. Timber, both hardwood and softwood, serves as a fundamental building block for the construction and furniture industries. Non-timber forest products (NTFPs) offer everything from fruits, nuts, and mushrooms to medicinal plants and resins, providing sustenance and income opportunities for communities.

Beyond these tangible benefits, forests play an indispensable role in regulating local climates. They act as sponges, soaking up rainfall and slowly releasing it. This regulation helps mitigate the risks of floods and droughts, contributing to the overall stability of ecosystems.

Moreover, forests enhance air and water quality, filtering pollutants and providing clean water to countless communities downstream. These ecosystem services, often overlooked, are vital for human well-being and the nation's ecological health.

**The Unique Challenges Facing Anambra State**

Anambra State, nestled in the southeastern part of Nigeria, possesses its own share of forested landscapes. Each reserve boasts its own unique character and ecological significance. Anambra State, with a population of approximately 5.5 million people and a land area of about 4,844 square kilometers, boasts forests that cover around 20% of its land. These forests offer a multitude of goods and services to both the populace and the environment. However, they also confront distinct challenges, including:

1. Loss of Forest Reserves: Forest reserves, designated areas legally safeguarded and managed for the sustainable utilization and conservation of forest resources, play a vital role in Anambra State. Currently, the state encompasses 12 forest reserves, spanning approximately 60,000 hectares. Unfortunately, these reserves are diminishing at an alarming rate of 3.5% annually due to encroachments, excisions, and outright de-reservations. A notable case study in the Apakah Forest Reserve reveals a staggering loss of about 90% of its original area since 1976. This decline has far-reaching environmental repercussions, including erosion, flooding, shifts in local climate conditions, stream siltation, and the endangerment of plant and animal species.

2. Ineffective Forest Governance and Policy Implementation: Effective forest governance involves the establishment of rules, institutions, processes, and practices that govern forest management. Forest policy, on the other hand, sets forth objectives, principles, and instruments to guide forest management. While Anambra State enacted a forest policy act in 2006, its implementation remains virtually nonexistent at both the state and local government levels, existing primarily on paper. Corruption, ignorance, insecurity, population growth, urban expansion, and excessive consumption further exacerbate the depletion of forest reserves. Stakeholders have underscored the necessity for enhanced collaboration and community participation to combat deforestation and forest degradation, not only within Anambra State but throughout Nigeria.

3. Low Awareness and Underestimation of Forest Resources: A considerable portion of the population in Anambra State lacks awareness of the value and significance of forests for their livelihoods and overall well-being. Additionally, many fail to grasp the broader societal and economic benefits that forests offer. Forests, for instance, play a pivotal role in carbon sequestration, aiding in climate change mitigation. They also supply timber, fuelwood, non-timber forest products (NTFPs), ecosystem services, and cultural values to local communities. Unfortunately, these goods and services are frequently undervalued or not priced adequately in the market, leading to overexploitation and the depreciation of forest resources.

To address these pressing challenges, several potential solutions can be pursued:

1. Development of a Sustainable Forest Management Model: A sustainable forest management (SFM) model has been formulated for Anambra State, emphasizing factors such as community involvement, awareness promotion, effective forest policy implementation, staff training, and the categorization of forest reserve loss into three phases (input, throughput, and output). SFM aims to manage forests in a manner that meets present needs without compromising the ability of future generations to fulfill their own requirements.

2. Enforcement of Laws and Regulations: Strengthening the enforcement of laws and regulations to safeguard forests against illegal activities like logging, mining, farming, and encroachments is paramount. Stringent penalties for violators, along with incentives for compliance, must be implemented. Additionally, transparency and accountability should be ensured in the allocation and management of forest resources.

3. Promotion of Alternative Livelihoods: To alleviate the reliance of individuals on forests for their income, alternative livelihood options should be promoted. This may involve granting access to credit, markets, education, healthcare, and other social services. Supporting initiatives like agroforestry, ecotourism, non-timber forest products (NTFPs), and other income-generating activities that align with forest conservation objectives can contribute significantly to addressing these challenges.

However, amid the natural beauty and ecological richness, Anambra State grapples with a set of unique challenges. One of the most pressing concerns is deforestation, which is evident right from the roads leading to the reserve areas. Here, firewood and timber are displayed for sale on both sides, a stark reminder of the relentless pace of forest loss.

Deforestation is driven by various factors, including the demand for timber and wood products, agricultural expansion, and population growth. The consequences are far-reaching, affecting not only the ecological equilibrium but also the livelihoods of communities dependent on forest resources.

Indiscriminate logging further exacerbates the problem. Without proper regulation and sustainable management, forests are vulnerable to exploitation, which can lead to habitat destruction, soil erosion, and loss of biodiversity. These challenges underscore the urgent need for robust and sustainable forest management practices in Anambra State.

In conclusion, Anambra State's forests are facing formidable challenges that necessitate immediate attention. Implementing these solutions can enhance sustainable forest management, preserve forest resources, and ensure that the rich ecological and economic benefits of forests continue to enrich the lives of current and future generations in the state.

## The Interconnectedness of Forests and Water Resources

Within the realm of sustainable forestry practices, it is imperative to recognize the profound interconnectedness between forests and water resources. Forests are not isolated entities but integral components of the broader hydrological cycle.

Forests, especially those in the upper reaches of watersheds, play a pivotal role in maintaining water quality and quantity. They act as natural sponges, absorbing rainfall and gradually releasing it into rivers and streams. This regulation of water flow mitigates the risks of floods during heavy rainfall and ensures a steady supply of water during dry seasons, safeguarding communities downstream.

Moreover, forests serve as guardians against soil erosion, preventing sediment from entering water bodies and disrupting aquatic ecosystems. The health of Nigeria's rivers, lakes, and wetlands is intrinsically tied to the preservation of its forests.

Forests also contribute to the overall quality of water. The intricate root systems of trees help filter pollutants from runoff, ensuring that the water that flows through forested landscapes is cleaner and less contaminated. This is not only essential for aquatic life but also for the communities that rely on these water sources for drinking and irrigation.

In Anambra State, the conservation of forests holds the key to safeguarding the state's water resources. The interconnectedness between these two natural systems underscores the importance of sustainable forest management in ensuring a stable and clean water supply for communities.

## Conclusion

Nigeria's forests, from the tropical rainforests of the south to the savannas of the north, are a source of immense pride and ecological significance. They provide invaluable resources, support biodiversity, regulate local climates, and contribute to the nation's economy.

In Anambra State, where forests are both a source of wonder and a challenge, the need for sustainable forest management is pressing. Deforestation and indiscriminate logging pose threats to the state's natural heritage and the well-being of its communities. The interconnectedness between forests and water resources underscores the importance of responsible forest stewardship.

As we continue our exploration, we will delve into strategies and initiatives that hold the promise of conserving these invaluable natural assets for future generations. The journey towards sustainable forestry practices is not without its challenges, but it is a journey worth embarking upon for the preservation of Nigeria's forests and the prosperity of its people.

CHAPTER 8

## Challenges and Threats to Anambra's Forests

The forests of Anambra State, like many natural landscapes around the world, face a myriad of challenges and threats that compromise their ecological integrity and long-term sustainability. In this chapter, we turn our attention to the complex web of factors driving deforestation in the state, including the relentless forces of agricultural expansion, the allure of timber-related income, and the shadowy world of illegal activities that cast a dark cloud over the state's forests.

## Deforestation Drivers in Anambra State

Deforestation is a multifaceted issue, often driven by a combination of socioeconomic, cultural, and environmental factors. In the case of Anambra State, several key drivers stand out, each contributing to the gradual loss of its precious forested landscapes.

1. Agricultural Expansion: One of the primary drivers of deforestation in Anambra State is agricultural expansion. As the population grows and the demand for food and agricultural products increases, farmers often find themselves clearing forests to create arable land for crops and pasture for

livestock. The allure of fertile soil and the promise of increased agricultural yields are powerful motivators.

The conversion of forests into agricultural land is a double-edged sword. While it meets the immediate needs for food production, it comes at the cost of irreplaceable biodiversity and the essential ecosystem services that forests provide, including water regulation and carbon sequestration.

2. Logging: Timber is a valuable and marketable resource in Anambra State, offering a source of income for many individuals and communities. While responsible and sustainable logging practices are possible, illegal logging is a prevalent issue. Some individuals and entities exploit forests without regard for long-term consequences, leading to deforestation, habitat destruction, and soil degradation.

Logging, when conducted without proper oversight and sustainable management, can have devastating effects on forest ecosystems. It disrupts habitats, threatens wildlife, and contributes to soil erosion, which can result in landslides and decreased water quality.

3. Illegal Activities: The clandestine world of illegal activities further exacerbates deforestation in Anambra State. Two prominent illegal activities include bush burning and charcoal production. Desperate for livelihoods, some individuals turn to these practices as a means of survival.

Bush burning is often employed to clear land for agricultural purposes quickly, but it has severe consequences for forest ecosystems. The intense heat can destroy not only trees but also the seeds and microorganisms in the soil, making forest regeneration difficult.

Charcoal production, too, takes a toll on forests. Charcoal is a valuable commodity, and its production involves the cutting and burning of wood. This practice, when unregulated, contributes significantly to deforestation.

**The Impact of Agricultural Expansion**

Agricultural expansion, driven by population growth and food security concerns, is a major driver of deforestation not only in Anambra State but also globally. As the demand for food, crops, and livestock rises, the conversion of forests into agricultural land becomes increasingly common.

While this expansion can alleviate immediate food security challenges, it often results in long-term ecological consequences. Forests are vital in regulating local climates, conserving biodiversity, and preserving water resources. Their loss can lead to soil degradation, decreased water quality, and disrupted hydrological cycles, impacting both the environment and communities downstream.

Moreover, the clearance of forests for agriculture releases stored carbon dioxide into the atmosphere, contributing to global climate change. Sustainable land-use practices that balance agricultural needs with forest conservation are essential to mitigate these adverse effects.

## Logging and Illegal Activities

Logging, particularly when undertaken illegally or unsustainably, poses a significant threat to Anambra State's forests. Timber is a valuable resource that offers economic opportunities to communities and individuals. However, the unregulated extraction of timber can lead to severe ecological and socioeconomic consequences.

Illegal logging not only damages forests but also undermines legal and sustainable logging operations. It deprives governments of revenue, threatens the livelihoods of communities dependent on forest resources, and exacerbates deforestation.

Illegal activities like bush burning and charcoal production further compound the issue. While these activities may provide short-term economic relief for individuals, they exact a heavy toll on the environment. Forests that are subjected to uncontrolled fires and extensive charcoal production struggle to regenerate, leading to long-term ecological degradation.

## Conclusion

The challenges and threats facing Anambra State's forests are complex and multifaceted. Deforestation, driven by agricultural expansion, logging, and illegal activities, poses a significant risk to the state's ecological balance, biodiversity, and the well-being of its communities.

Addressing these challenges requires a multi-pronged approach that involves sustainable land-use practices, responsible forest management, and robust enforcement of forestry regulations. It also necessitates community engagement and awareness-raising to promote the value of forests and the importance of their preservation.

As we move forward in our exploration, we will delve into strategies and initiatives aimed at mitigating these threats and fostering a harmonious coexistence between Anambra State's people and its invaluable forests.

CHAPTER 9

## Strategies for Sustainable Forest Management in Anambra State

Anambra State, like many regions grappling with deforestation and the depletion of forest resources, faces a pivotal moment in its history. The preservation and sustainable management of its forests are not just ecological imperatives but also essential for the well-being and livelihoods of its communities. In this chapter, we delve deeper into strategies that can chart a path towards sustainable forest management, focusing on the critical role of local communities, the potential of reforestation and afforestation programs, and the importance of promoting sustainable agricultural practices.

## Local Community Involvement and Empowerment

The forests of Anambra State have long been intertwined with the lives and cultures of its people. The state's communities have relied on forest resources for their sustenance, building materials, and cultural practices for generations. Acknowledging the central role of local communities in sustainable forest management is not just a necessity; it is an opportunity to leverage their knowledge, traditions, and commitment to the preservation of these vital ecosystems.

## 1. Empowerment through Education

Empowering local communities with knowledge and awareness is a foundational step in sustainable forest management. Education programs can be designed to inform communities about the ecological importance of forests, the benefits of sustainable practices, and the potential for alternative livelihoods. These programs aim to create a shift in mindset, helping communities recognize the long-term advantages of forest conservation.

In Anambra State, community education can take the form of workshops, seminars, and awareness campaigns. Topics may include forest ecology, the value of biodiversity, responsible resource harvesting, and sustainable income-generating activities that reduce dependency on forests.

## 2. Community-Based Forest Management

An effective approach to sustainable forest management involves engaging local communities directly in the stewardship of nearby forests. Community-based forest management empowers these communities with legal rights and responsibilities for managing and benefiting from forest resources sustainably.

In such systems, decision-making processes are participatory, ensuring that communities have a say in how the forests are managed. This approach not only aligns with principles of justice and equity but also promotes responsible resource utilization.

## 3. Sustainable Livelihoods

Sustainable forest management should not solely focus on the conservation of forests but also on the improvement of the well-being of local communities. Initiatives that promote sustainable livelihoods can help alleviate the economic pressure on forests and reduce dependency.

In Anambra State, several income-generating activities can be integrated into sustainable forest management plans. Non-timber forest product harvesting, such as gathering medicinal plants, nuts, and fruits, can offer alternative income sources. Additionally, eco-tourism initiatives that showcase the state's natural beauty and biodiversity can stimulate local economies while preserving the forests.

These strategies collectively empower local communities to become stewards of their forests, not merely as a source of resources but as a critical component of their cultural heritage and ecological legacy.

## Reforestation and Afforestation Programs

The restoration of degraded forests and the expansion of forested areas are pivotal in the pursuit of sustainable forest management in Anambra State. Reforestation and afforestation programs represent concrete steps toward revitalizing the state's forest ecosystems.

1. Reforestation

Reforestation is a focused effort to restore areas that have been deforested or degraded. It involves the deliberate planting of trees, often native species that are well-suited to the local environment. In Anambra State, identifying suitable sites for reforestation is essential.

Areas that have been subjected to logging, bush burning, or other forms of degradation should be prioritized for reforestation. The choice of tree species should consider ecological compatibility and the potential for biodiversity enhancement.

2. Afforestation

Afforestation goes a step further by creating forests in areas that were not previously forested. This proactive approach to expanding forest cover is critical for mitigating the impacts of deforestation and habitat loss. In Anambra State, afforestation efforts should align with local environmental conditions and long-term sustainability goals.

Strategic planning plays a significant role in the success of afforestation programs. Identifying areas suitable for afforestation, securing appropriate land tenure arrangements, and involving local communities in the planting and maintenance of new forests are essential considerations.

## Promoting Sustainable Agricultural Practices

The intricate relationship between agriculture and deforestation underscores the importance of promoting sustainable agricultural practices. By reducing the pressure on forests, while simultaneously enhancing the livelihoods of farmers, Anambra State can achieve a harmonious coexistence between agriculture and forest conservation.

1. Agroforestry

Agroforestry is a sustainable land-use practice that integrates trees and crops on the same land. This approach offers multiple benefits, both to farmers and the environment. Trees in agroforestry systems can improve soil fertility, protect against erosion, and provide additional income sources through the sale of timber or non-timber forest products.

Promoting agroforestry practices in Anambra State can be a win-win solution. Local farmers can diversify their income sources while contributing to the conservation of forests and enhancing ecological resilience.

## 2. Sustainable Land Use Planning

Effective land use planning is crucial for reconciling agriculture and forest conservation. An integrated approach that zones areas for agriculture, reforestation, and protected conservation can help strike a balance between the needs of both sectors.

Collaboration between agricultural and environmental agencies is essential to ensure that land use planning aligns with the broader goals of sustainable forest management. This cooperation can lead to the designation of forest reserves and the enforcement of sustainable land-use practices.

## 3. Forest-Friendly Farming Techniques

Promoting forest-friendly farming techniques can mitigate the negative impacts of agriculture on forests. Techniques such as reduced-impact logging, which minimize the ecological footprint of logging activities, and no-till agriculture, which reduces soil erosion and deforestation associated with land clearance, can be encouraged among local farmers.

Training and incentives can motivate farmers to adopt these practices. Support from government agencies and non-governmental organizations can be instrumental in implementing and promoting sustainable farming techniques.

## Conclusion

The journey toward sustainable forest management in Anambra State is multifaceted and challenging, but it is also profoundly rewarding. Local community involvement and empowerment, reforestation and afforestation programs, and the promotion of sustainable agricultural practices are fundamental components of this transformative journey.

By embracing these strategies, Anambra State cannot only safeguard its invaluable forests but also secure the well-being of its communities, protect biodiversity, and contribute to climate change mitigation. The path ahead may be daunting, but the prospect of a harmonious coexistence between people and forests is a vision worth pursuing. In doing so, Anambra State can set an example of sustainable forest management for generations to come.

CHAPTER 10

**Policy and Governance**

Sustainable forestry is not solely a task for individual actors or communities—it necessitates effective policy and governance mechanisms at various levels of government. In this chapter, we delve into the pivotal role of government in sustainable forestry, the significance of legal frameworks and enforcement, and the crucial importance of cross-sectoral collaboration.

**Role of Forest Guards**

Forest guards, also known as forest rangers or forest protectors, play a crucial role in safeguarding and managing forests and natural resources. Their duties may vary depending on the specific responsibilities assigned by their employing agency or organization, but here are some common duties of forest guards:

1. Patrolling: Forest guards are responsible for patrolling designated forest areas to monitor activities and check for any signs of illegal logging, poaching, encroachments, or other unauthorized activities. Regular patrols help deter illegal activities and ensure compliance with forest conservation laws.

2. Wildlife Protection: Forest guards protect wildlife and their habitats by preventing poaching, monitoring endangered species, and ensuring the safety of wildlife in the forest. They may participate in efforts to conserve and rehabilitate wildlife populations.

3. Fire Prevention and Management: Forest guards are often involved in fire prevention and management activities. They help prevent forest fires by enforcing fire safety regulations, conducting controlled burns, and educating the public on fire prevention. In case of a forest fire, they may coordinate firefighting efforts.

4. Illegal Logging and Timber Theft: Forest guards combat illegal logging and timber theft by inspecting logging operations, verifying the legality of timber harvesting, and ensuring loggers adhere to regulations. They also monitor the transportation of timber to prevent illegal trade.

5. Community Engagement: Forest guards work closely with local communities that live near or within forest areas. They promote awareness of conservation efforts, involve communities in sustainable forest management practices, and address conflicts related to natural resource use.

6. Data Collection and Reporting: Forest guards collect data on forest health, wildlife populations, and illegal activities. They maintain records, prepare reports, and share information with relevant authorities to support decision-making and law enforcement efforts.

7. Enforcement of Laws and Regulations: Forest guards have the authority to enforce forest and environmental laws. They may issue

warnings, citations, or take legal action against individuals or entities involved in illegal activities within the forest.

8. Habitat Restoration: Some forest guards participate in habitat restoration activities, such as planting trees, controlling invasive species, and rehabilitating degraded areas to enhance biodiversity and ecosystem health.

9. Emergency Response: Forest guards may be called upon to respond to emergencies within the forest, including accidents, medical emergencies, or search and rescue operations.

10. Education and Outreach: They educate visitors, tourists, and local communities about the importance of forest conservation and sustainable resource management. This includes guiding nature tours and conducting educational programs.

11. Equipment Maintenance: Forest guards are responsible for maintaining their equipment, such as vehicles, communication devices, and safety gear, to ensure they are prepared for their duties.

12. Collaboration: They collaborate with other law enforcement agencies, conservation organizations, and government departments to address broader environmental and wildlife protection issues.

It's important to note that the specific duties of forest guards can vary based on their location, the size and importance of the forested area, and the policies and regulations in place. Their work is vital in preserving and protecting the world's forests and the biodiversity they contain.

**Urgent need for the employment of more forest guards to protect valuable forest resources**

The urgent need for the employment of more forest guards to protect valuable forest resources across the federation is a critical concern for the preservation of our natural heritage. Forests play a crucial role in maintaining ecological balance, providing livelihoods, conserving biodiversity, and mitigating climate change. However, they face numerous threats, including illegal logging, wildlife poaching, encroachments, and habitat degradation.

**Here are some key reasons highlighting the urgency of employing more forest guards:**

1. Illegal Activities: Forests are vulnerable to illegal activities such as illegal logging, timber theft, and wildlife poaching. Without sufficient forest guards, these activities can continue unabated, leading to the depletion of valuable resources.

2. Biodiversity Conservation: Forests are home to diverse plant and animal species, many of which are endangered or endemic. More forest guards are needed to protect these species from poachers and habitat destruction.

3. Deforestation: Deforestation and forest degradation contribute to climate change. Adequate forest guards can help monitor and enforce regulations to prevent deforestation and promote reforestation.

4. Community Livelihoods: Forests provide livelihoods for many local communities through sustainable forest management and non-timber forest products. Protecting these resources ensures the economic well-being of forest-dependent communities.

5. Environmental Services: Forests provide essential ecosystem services such as clean water, air purification, and soil stabilization. Increased protection of forests safeguards these services.

6. Global Commitments: Nigeria has international commitments to protect its forests, such as the United Nations' Sustainable Development Goals (SDGs) and global climate agreements. Adequate forest protection is essential to meet these commitments.

7. Conflict Resolution: Forest guards can play a role in resolving conflicts related to resource use between different stakeholders, including communities, loggers, and conservationists.

8. Fire Prevention: Forest fires pose a significant threat to forest ecosystems. More forest guards can help implement fire prevention strategies and respond to fire emergencies promptly.

9. Data Collection: Forest guards collect valuable data on forest health and illegal activities. This data is essential for evidence-based decision-making and policy formulation.

10. Education and Awareness: Forest guards can engage with local communities and raise awareness about the importance of forest conservation. They can also provide training on sustainable forest management practices.

To address this urgent need, governments, non-governmental organizations, and relevant authorities should prioritize the recruitment, training, and deployment of additional forest guards. Adequate funding, resources, and logistical support should be provided to enable them to carry out their duties effectively.

Furthermore, collaboration between different stakeholders, including local communities, is crucial to ensuring the sustainable protection of our forests. Together, we can safeguard our valuable forest resources for current and future generations.

**The Role of Government in Sustainable Forestry**

Governments, at both the national and regional levels, play a foundational role in shaping the trajectory of sustainable forestry within their jurisdictions. Their responsibilities encompass crafting policies, providing regulatory frameworks, and facilitating the coordination of efforts among diverse stakeholders.

Governor Charles Soludo, the incumbent leader of Anambra State since November 6, 2021, brings a wealth of expertise as a former Governor of the Central Bank of Nigeria, a distinguished economist, and a respected academic. His tenure has been marked by commendable efforts aimed at preserving and nurturing the forests of Anambra State. His vision and commitment to safeguarding these natural treasures are worthy of recognition and tribute.

Here are some of the notable initiatives undertaken by Governor Chukwuma Soludo:

1. The Anambra Green Project: A transformative initiative launched on November 17, 2021, the Anambra Green Project is a collaborative effort involving the state government, the Nigeria Erosion and Watershed Management Project (NEWMAP), and the World Bank. This ambitious endeavor sets out to plant an impressive 10 million trees across the state by 2025. The project's multifaceted goals encompass combatting deforestation, mitigating erosion, preventing flooding, addressing climate change, and improving the overall livelihoods and well-being of the people of Anambra State. Governor Soludo's leadership in spearheading this project underscores his dedication to environmental sustainability and the welfare of the populace.

2. Need for Establishment of the Anambra State Forest Commission: Under Governor Soludo's leadership, Anambra State would take a significant step forward in forest management with the creation of the Anambra State Forest Commission. When established in accordance with the Anambra State Laws would align with the global efforts towards sustainable development and biodiversity conservation. This pioneering agency would assume responsibility for formulating, implementing, and coordinating policies and programs aimed at conserving and sustainably managing the state's forest resources. Additionally, the commission would play a pivotal role in overseeing the regulation, monitoring, and enforcement of forest-related laws and regulations. This institutional framework would further underscore Governor Soludo's commitment to effective forest governance.

3. Support for Community-Based Forest Management (CBFM): Recognizing the importance of local communities in preserving and

managing forests, Governor Soludo has championed the cause of Community-Based Forest Management (CBFM). This approach empowers and engages local communities in forest management activities. Under his leadership, the state has provided incentives, capacity-building initiatives, and technical assistance to Community Forest Associations (CFAs) throughout Anambra State. Moreover, Governor Soludo has encouraged the integration of indigenous knowledge and traditional practices into forest management strategies. His support for CBFM underscores the importance of local participation and indigenous wisdom in sustainable forest management.

In paying tribute to His Excellency Prof. Charles Chukwuma Soludo, we acknowledge his remarkable vision and unwavering commitment to the protection and enhancement of Anambra State's forests. His leadership not only serves the interests of the present generation but also lays the groundwork for a more sustainable and prosperous future for the people and the environment of Anambra State.

1. Policy Formulation: Governments have the authority to establish comprehensive policies that set the direction for sustainable forestry practices. These policies often incorporate environmental, social, and economic objectives, emphasizing the need to balance conservation with livelihoods and economic growth.

2. Legal Frameworks: Legal frameworks are instrumental in translating policy objectives into actionable guidelines. Laws and regulations can define sustainable forest management practices, land-use planning, and resource allocation. They also create a foundation for monitoring and enforcement.

3. Funding Support: Governments can allocate financial resources to support sustainable forestry initiatives. This funding can be directed towards reforestation and afforestation programs, research and development, capacity building, and monitoring efforts. Financial incentives can encourage private and community involvement in forest conservation.

**Legal Frameworks and Enforcement**

Legal frameworks underpin sustainable forestry practices and provide a framework for compliance. These frameworks are designed to ensure that forests are managed sustainably and that the rights of local communities are protected. Effective enforcement mechanisms are crucial to ensuring that these legal frameworks are adhered to.

1. Regulatory Clarity: Clear and comprehensive regulations help define what constitutes sustainable forest management. They specify logging practices, protected areas, conservation measures, and community engagement requirements. Clarity is vital for both forest managers and law enforcement agencies.

2. Monitoring and Surveillance: Robust monitoring and surveillance systems are indispensable for enforcing forestry regulations. Technology, such as satellite imagery and remote sensing, can aid in tracking deforestation, illegal logging, and encroachments into protected areas.

3. Law Enforcement: Strong enforcement mechanisms are essential for deterring illegal activities and holding violators accountable. This may involve forest rangers, law enforcement agencies, and penalties for violations. Public awareness campaigns can also foster a culture of compliance.

**The Importance of Cross-Sectoral Collaboration**

Sustainable forest management does not occur in isolation; it thrives when different sectors work in harmony to achieve shared goals. Collaboration across sectors, such as agriculture, forestry, and tourism, can create synergies that promote sustainable forest management practices.

1. Intersectoral Coordination: Collaboration between government departments responsible for forestry, agriculture, environment, and tourism is vital. Coordinated efforts can help align policies, share resources, and avoid conflicts of interest that may threaten forests.

2. Integrated Land Use Planning: Integrated land use planning considers multiple sectors when allocating land for different purposes. This approach can help ensure that forests are conserved while allowing for

responsible agricultural expansion, sustainable tourism, and other land uses.

3. Community Engagement: Collaboration extends to local communities, who are often at the forefront of sustainable forestry practices. Engaging communities in decision-making processes, respecting their rights, and recognizing their roles as stewards of the land can foster collective responsibility for forest conservation.

4. Research and Innovation: Cross-sectoral collaboration can also stimulate innovation and knowledge sharing. Research institutions, universities, and non-governmental organizations can play a pivotal role in advancing sustainable forestry practices through research, education, and the dissemination of best practices.

In conclusion, policy and governance are foundational pillars of sustainable forestry. Government policies and legal frameworks guide sustainable practices, while enforcement mechanisms ensure compliance. Cross-sectoral collaboration harnesses the strengths of different sectors and communities to achieve shared objectives.

Through effective governance, legal frameworks, and cross-sectoral collaboration, Anambra State and regions facing similar challenges can foster a harmonious coexistence between forests and the various sectors that rely on them. Ultimately, it is through these concerted efforts that sustainable forestry practices can thrive, securing a sustainable future for all.

CHAPTER 11

## The Economic Potential of Sustainable Forestry in Anambra State

The economic potential of sustainable forestry in Anambra State is immense and multifaceted. In this chapter, we explore the substantial economic benefits of sustainable forest management, emphasizing the pivotal role of eco-tourism as a driving force for local economies. We also delve into case studies of successful initiatives, shedding light on the transformative power of sustainable forestry practices.

## Economic Benefits of Sustainable Forest Management

Sustainable forest management in Anambra State offers a spectrum of economic benefits, not only for local communities but also for the broader region and the state as a whole.

1. Timber Resources: Sustainable logging practices provide a consistent supply of timber, a valuable resource for various industries such as construction, furniture manufacturing, and crafts. Revenue generated from timber sales can contribute significantly to local and state economies.

2. Non-Timber Forest Products (NTFPs): Forests are treasure troves of non-timber products, including fruits, nuts, mushrooms, medicinal plants, and resins. These resources not only supplement the income of forest-dependent communities but also offer opportunities for trade and economic diversification.

3. Eco-Tourism: The pristine natural beauty and biodiversity of Anambra State's forests are a draw for eco-tourists seeking unique experiences. Sustainable eco-tourism initiatives can stimulate local economies by attracting visitors, generating income for communities, and fostering a sense of pride in forest conservation.

4. Carbon Sequestration: Forests' capacity to sequester carbon dioxide has economic implications on a global scale. As international efforts to combat climate change intensify, Anambra State's well-managed forests may provide opportunities for carbon offset credits, which can generate additional revenue.

## The Role of Eco-Tourism

Eco-tourism stands as a powerful catalyst for sustainable forest management, offering a symbiotic relationship between nature conservation and economic prosperity.

1. Community Engagement: Eco-tourism can directly involve local communities in the tourism value chain, from providing accommodations

and guiding services to selling local products. This engagement creates jobs and additional income streams, reducing reliance on unsustainable forest practices.

2. Cultural Exchange: Anambra State's forests are rich in cultural heritage, providing opportunities for tourists to engage with local traditions and customs. Cultural experiences not only enhance the tourism offering but also foster a deeper appreciation for the forests' significance.

3. Conservation Funding: The revenue generated from eco-tourism can be reinvested into forest conservation efforts. This financial support can fund monitoring, anti-poaching measures, and reforestation projects, ensuring the long-term health of the forests.

**Case Studies of Successful Initiatives**

Learning from the experiences of successful initiatives can provide valuable insights into the economic potential of sustainable forestry in Anambra State.

1. Eco-Tourism in Achalla Forest Reserve: The Achalla Forest Reserve, with its diverse flora and fauna, has become a hub for eco-tourism. Local communities offer guided tours, accommodations, and cultural experiences, attracting tourists from far and wide. The revenue generated from eco-tourism has bolstered the local economy while safeguarding the reserve.

2. Non-Timber Forest Products Cooperatives: Anambra State has witnessed the emergence of cooperatives focused on non-timber forest products. These cooperatives facilitate sustainable harvesting, processing, and marketing of products such as medicinal herbs and nuts. By creating value-added products and accessing larger markets, these initiatives have improved the economic prospects of communities.

3. Reforestation and Carbon Credit Sales: Anambra State's commitment to reforestation has attracted international attention. Successful reforestation projects have resulted in carbon sequestration credits that are sold on international markets. The revenue generated is reinvested in forest management and community development.

## Conclusion

Sustainable forest management in Anambra State holds immense economic potential, offering a sustainable path to prosperity for local communities and the state. Timber resources, non-timber forest products, and eco-tourism are key economic drivers, while initiatives like carbon credit sales provide additional revenue streams.

By embracing sustainable forestry practices and nurturing eco-tourism, Anambra State cannot only preserve its natural heritage but also fuel economic growth, enhance livelihoods, and contribute to global efforts to combat climate change. The case studies of successful initiatives underscore the feasibility and transformative power of sustainable forestry in the state. The economic potential is not merely a promise but a reality that can be realized through wise stewardship of Anambra State's forests.

CHAPTER 12

## Education and Awareness

Education and awareness form the bedrock of sustainable forest management. In this chapter, we delve into the compelling need for public awareness campaigns, the critical role of environmental education in schools, and the transformative journey toward building a culture of forest conservation.

## The Need for Public Awareness Campaigns

Public awareness campaigns serve as powerful tools to communicate the significance of forests and promote sustainable forest management practices. These campaigns aim to inform, engage, and inspire individuals and communities to take action for the preservation of forests.

1. Raising Awareness: Public awareness campaigns are instrumental in disseminating information about forests' vital roles in ecosystem health, climate regulation, and the global economy. They highlight the threats facing forests and the consequences of unsustainable practices.

2. Fostering Engagement: Effective campaigns engage individuals and communities in the discourse on forest conservation. They encourage people to become active participants in safeguarding forests through sustainable actions and responsible consumption.

3. Advocating for Change: Public awareness campaigns can catalyze advocacy efforts, encouraging citizens to influence policy decisions and hold businesses and governments accountable for their forest-related practices.

**Environmental Education in Schools**

Environmental education plays a pivotal role in nurturing a generation of environmentally conscious citizens. Integrating forest conservation principles into school curricula can have a profound and lasting impact on future generations.

1. Early Learning: Introducing children to the wonders of forests at an early age kindles their curiosity and sense of wonder. Simple activities, such as nature walks and tree planting, can instill a lifelong appreciation for forests.

2. Holistic Understanding: Environmental education in schools provides students with a holistic understanding of the interconnections between

forests, biodiversity, climate, and human well-being. It equips them with the knowledge and skills to make informed decisions about forest conservation.

3. Empowering Action: Schools can inspire students to take action in their communities. Environmental clubs, tree-planting initiatives, and awareness campaigns led by students can drive positive change at the local level.

## Building a Culture of Forest Conservation

A culture of forest conservation entails integrating sustainable forest management practices into the daily lives of individuals and communities. It goes beyond knowledge and awareness, encompassing values, attitudes, and behaviors that prioritize forests.

1. Sustainable Lifestyles: Encouraging sustainable consumption patterns, such as choosing certified wood products and supporting responsible brands, can foster a culture of forest-friendly choices.

2. Community Engagement: Empowering local communities to become stewards of their forests reinforces a culture of conservation. Involving communities in decision-making and benefiting from forest resources sustainably deepens their commitment to conservation.

3. Celebrating Forests: Marking events like International Day of Forests can create opportunities to celebrate the intrinsic value of forests and reinforce their importance in our lives.

## Examples of Successful Public Awareness Campaigns

Several initiatives have successfully raised awareness about sustainable forestry and the need for responsible consumption.

1. Forest Stewardship Council (FSC): The FSC is an international certification system that promotes responsible forest management. Its iconic logo on wood products informs consumers that the product is sourced from sustainably managed forests.

2. Roundtable on Sustainable Palm Oil (RSPO): RSPO is a certification system that promotes the production and use of sustainable palm oil. It has raised awareness about the environmental and social impacts of palm oil production and encourages consumers to choose sustainable palm oil products.

## Conclusion

Education and awareness are the cornerstones of sustainable forest management. Public awareness campaigns bridge the gap between knowledge and action, inspiring individuals and communities to champion forest conservation. Environmental education in schools lays the foundation for a generation that values and safeguards forests. Building a culture of forest conservation ensures that sustainable practices endure, securing the future of forests for generations to come.

In the journey toward sustainable forest management, education and awareness are not mere components but catalysts for transformative change. They empower individuals to become advocates for forests, advocates for our shared future.

CHAPTER 13

## Challenges and Solutions

As we navigate the path of sustainable forest management, we encounter a range of challenges that demand innovative solutions. In this chapter, we explore strategies for overcoming resistance to change, addressing short-term economic pressures, and mobilizing the necessary resources for effective implementation.

## Overcoming Resistance to Change

Resistance to change is a natural reaction when transitioning to sustainable forest management practices. It can emanate from various quarters, including local communities, government officials, and industry stakeholders. Overcoming this resistance is paramount for success.

1. Inclusive Decision-Making: Involving stakeholders in the decision-making process fosters a sense of ownership and inclusion. Consultations, dialogues, and participatory approaches ensure that diverse perspectives are considered, leading to more effective and acceptable solutions.

2. Education and Training: Providing training and support to those directly affected by changes in forest management practices can alleviate fears and build capacity. Training programs can equip communities and industry professionals with the skills needed to adapt to sustainable practices.

3. Communicating Benefits: Effectively communicating the long-term benefits of sustainable forest management is crucial. Highlighting improved livelihoods, healthier ecosystems, and economic stability can help stakeholders understand the advantages of change.

## Addressing Short-Term Economic Pressures

Short-term economic pressures often drive unsustainable forest management practices. It is essential to find ways to reconcile immediate economic needs with the long-term benefits of forests.

1. Diversification of Income Sources: Encouraging local communities to diversify their income sources can help reduce reliance on forest resources for immediate financial gain. Initiatives such as sustainable agriculture, eco-tourism, and non-timber forest products can provide alternative income streams.

2. Certification and Market Incentives: Promoting certified forest products in the market can create incentives for sustainable practices. Certifications like the Forest Stewardship Council (FSC) and others can command premium prices, providing economic benefits to producers.

3. Financial Incentives: Governments and organizations can provide financial incentives to support sustainable forest management. These incentives can include grants, subsidies, and low-interest loans to help offset the short-term economic challenges of transitioning to sustainable practices.

**Mobilizing Resources for Implementation**

Effective implementation of sustainable forest management practices requires the mobilization of resources, including funding, expertise, and community support.

1. Public and Private Partnerships: Collaboration between government agencies, private organizations, and local communities can leverage resources and expertise. Public-private partnerships can pool funds and knowledge to support sustainable initiatives.

2. International Aid and Grants: International organizations and donor agencies often provide funding for sustainable forest management projects. Accessing these resources can help bridge financial gaps and support implementation.

3. Capacity Building: Training and capacity-building programs can mobilize local communities to actively participate in sustainable forest management. By empowering communities with knowledge and skills, they become key contributors to implementation efforts.

**Conclusion**

The journey toward sustainable forest management is not without its challenges, but these challenges are not insurmountable. Overcoming resistance to change, addressing short-term economic pressures, and mobilizing resources are all essential components of a successful strategy.

By involving stakeholders, providing education and training, and effectively communicating the benefits of sustainable practices, we can navigate resistance to change. Diversifying income sources, promoting certifications, and providing financial incentives help address short-term economic pressures. Finally, forging partnerships, accessing international aid, and building local capacity are key to mobilizing the resources needed for implementation.

Sustainable forest management is a dynamic process that requires adaptability and resilience. With the right strategies and a collective commitment to the well-being of our forests, we can overcome challenges and secure a sustainable future for generations to come.

CHAPTER 14

## Monitoring and Evaluation

Monitoring and evaluation serve as the vigilant eyes and steady hands of sustainable forest management. In this chapter, we explore the critical roles of developing forest health indicators, tracking progress toward sustainability goals, and harnessing the power of technology in monitoring forest ecosystems.

## Developing Forest Health Indicators

Examples of forest health indicators encompass a wide range of factors that provide insights into the overall well-being and ecological condition of a forest ecosystem. These indicators help forest managers, researchers, and policymakers assess the health of forests and make informed decisions. Here are some examples of forest health indicators:

1. Post-Logging Woody Debris: The amount of woody debris left behind after timber extraction can be a critical indicator of forest health. An excessive accumulation of woody debris can impact nutrient cycling, obstruct regeneration, and increase the risk of wildfire.

2. Temperature: Monitoring temperature patterns within a forest can reveal shifts in climate and potential stress on plant and animal species. Temperature fluctuations can influence forest growth, insect infestations, and wildfire susceptibility.

3. Precipitation: Changes in precipitation patterns can have profound effects on forest health. Excessive or insufficient rainfall can impact soil moisture, affect tree growth, and contribute to drought stress or flooding events.

4. Fire Risk: Assessing the risk of wildfires is crucial for forest health. Indicators related to fire risk include factors like fuel load, moisture content, and historical fire frequency. Elevated fire risk can threaten both forest ecosystems and nearby communities.

5. Biotic Processes and Agents: Monitoring the presence and impact of biotic agents such as insects, fungi, and grazing animals is essential. Indicators may include the extent of insect outbreaks, the prevalence of specific fungal diseases, or the impact of overgrazing on forest understory vegetation.

6. Tree Health and Mortality: Tracking the condition of individual trees, including signs of stress, disease, or mortality, is a fundamental indicator of forest health. Unusually high tree mortality rates may indicate underlying issues such as drought or pest infestations.

7. Species Diversity: Assessing the diversity of plant and animal species within a forest is an indicator of its ecological resilience. Reduced species diversity may suggest environmental stress or habitat degradation.

8. Water Quality: The quality of water bodies within or downstream from a forest can serve as an indicator of its health. Elevated levels of pollutants or changes in water chemistry can signal environmental degradation.

9. Soil Health: Soil indicators, such as nutrient content, pH levels, and microbial activity, provide insights into the ability of the forest to support plant growth and maintain ecological functions.

10. Regeneration Success: Monitoring the successful establishment of new tree seedlings and other plant species following disturbances or logging activities is crucial. Poor regeneration can indicate problems with forest recovery.

11. Carbon Sequestration: Assessing the capacity of a forest to sequester carbon dioxide from the atmosphere is vital for climate change mitigation. Indicators may include changes in forest biomass and carbon storage.

12. Wildlife Abundance: Tracking the populations of key wildlife species within a forest can indicate the overall health of the ecosystem. Changes in abundance may reflect habitat quality and availability.

These forest health indicators are interconnected, and their interpretation often requires a comprehensive assessment that considers multiple factors simultaneously. Regular monitoring and analysis of these indicators help ensure the sustainability and resilience of forest ecosystems in the face of environmental challenges and management decisions.

Forest health indicators are the compass and barometer of sustainable forest management. They provide a structured framework for assessing the ecological, social, and economic well-being of forests. Developing these indicators is a meticulous process that involves identifying key parameters and metrics to measure the health and vitality of forests.

Ecological Indicators: These indicators gauge the biological and environmental aspects of forests, including biodiversity, tree health, water quality, and soil conditions. For example, the presence of specific plant and animal species can be used as indicators of ecosystem health.

Social Indicators: Social indicators assess the relationships between forests and communities, encompassing aspects like local employment, cultural significance, and stakeholder participation. Measuring the satisfaction and well-being of forest-dependent communities can be indicative of social sustainability.

Economic Indicators: Economic indicators focus on the financial aspects of forest management, such as revenue from timber sales, non-timber forest products, and ecotourism. These indicators help determine the economic viability of sustainable practices.

**Tracking Progress toward Sustainability Goals**

Sustainable forest management is an ongoing journey marked by clear goals and objectives. Tracking progress toward these sustainability goals is vital to ensure that management practices align with long-term aspirations.

Goal Setting: Establishing clear and measurable sustainability goals is the first step. These goals often revolve around maintaining or enhancing forest health, conserving biodiversity, supporting local livelihoods, and mitigating climate change.

**Regular Assessment: Regular assessments and audits of forest** health indicators provide insights into the progress made toward these goals. Monitoring the extent of forest regeneration, changes in species diversity, and the economic well-being of local communities are examples of such assessments.

Adaptive Management: The data collected through monitoring informs adaptive management strategies. If progress veers off track, adjustments can be made to management practices, policies, and conservation efforts to bring them back in line with sustainability goals.

**The Role of Technology in Monitoring**

Technology has revolutionized forest monitoring, enabling more accurate, efficient, and timely assessments. These technological tools offer a wealth of data and insights, enhancing our capacity to manage forests sustainably.

Remote Sensing: Satellite imagery, aerial drones, and other remote sensing technologies enable the regular observation of large forested areas. These tools can detect changes in forest cover, assess fire risks, and track the spread of pests and diseases.

Data Analytics: Advanced data analytics and modeling techniques help make sense of the vast amounts of data collected. They can identify trends, correlations, and potential issues, aiding decision-making processes.

Online Platforms: Online platforms and databases provide accessible repositories of forest health information. Stakeholders, including researchers, policymakers, and the public, can access and contribute to these platforms, fostering transparency and collaboration.

In this chapter, we've explored the pivotal roles of developing forest health indicators, tracking progress toward sustainability goals, and embracing technology in monitoring. These processes form the foundation of informed, adaptive, and effective sustainable forest management, ensuring that forests remain resilient, vibrant, and invaluable for generations to come.

-82-

CHAPTER 15

## Green and Sustainable Yield Goals

Green and sustainable yield goals stand as the compass guiding sustainable forest management practices. In this chapter, we delve into the essence of green and sustainable yield, the profound environmental imperative that underpins it, the delicate balance between economic and ecological objectives, and the vital consideration of social and cultural factors.

## Defining Green and Sustainable Yield

Green and sustainable yield is the heart of responsible forest management. It signifies the maximum harvest that does not deplete or over-harvest renewable resources to the point of irreversible damage. This principle lies at the intersection of economic prosperity, ecological vitality, and the preservation of cultural and social values.

## The Environmental Imperative

The environment is both the cradle and custodian of forests, and its health is intrinsically linked to green and sustainable yield goals. Sustainable forestry practices must prioritize the well-being of the environment, embracing several critical aspects:

Biodiversity Conservation: Forests are havens of biodiversity, and their preservation is vital for countless plant and animal species. Sustainable yield goals must ensure that forest ecosystems remain diverse and resilient.

Carbon Sequestration: Forests are powerful allies in the fight against climate change, sequestering carbon dioxide from the atmosphere. Sustainable yield practices must safeguard this capacity and contribute to climate change mitigation.

Ecosystem Health: Forest ecosystems offer a multitude of services, from regulating water flow to purifying the air. Sustainable forestry practices must maintain these services, supporting not only the forest itself but also the communities that depend on them.

## Balancing Economic and Ecological Objectives

Green and sustainable yield goals navigate the intricate interplay between economic prosperity and ecological stewardship. Achieving this equilibrium is paramount for ensuring that forests continue to provide economic benefits while also conserving their inherent value.

Long-Term Economic Benefits: Sustainable forest management recognizes that forests can provide economic returns over generations. By carefully harvesting and regenerating forests, sustainable practices offer the potential for enduring economic prosperity.

Ecosystem-Based Management: The concept of ecosystem-based management is central to green and sustainable yield goals. It emphasizes the holistic management of forest ecosystems, considering not just individual trees but the entire ecological web.

## Social and Cultural Considerations

Green and sustainable yield goals extend their reach to encompass the social and cultural fabric of forest-dependent communities. Sustainable forestry practices must respect the traditions, values, and needs of local communities.

Local Involvement: Sustainable forest management practices should actively engage with local communities, recognizing their role as stewards of the land. Involving communities in decision-making processes and benefit-sharing fosters a sense of ownership and responsibility.

Cultural Significance: Forests hold profound cultural significance for many communities. Sustainable forestry practices should honor and preserve cultural heritage, ensuring that forests continue to serve as places of spiritual and cultural importance.

Socioeconomic Benefits: Sustainable yield goals seek to support decent incomes for forest-dependent communities. This includes not only providing livelihood opportunities but also ensuring that these communities share in the economic benefits generated by forest resources.

In this chapter, we've navigated the intricate terrain of green and sustainable yield goals. These goals are more than just numbers; they are the embodiment of a harmonious relationship between humans and the natural world, where economic prosperity, ecological vitality, and cultural heritage thrive in unison.

CHAPTER 16

## Adapting Green and Sustainable Yield Goals to Anambra State's Forests

Bringing green and sustainable yield goals to fruition in the unique context of Anambra State demands a comprehensive approach. In this chapter, we embark on the journey of adaptation by assessing the state of Anambra's forests, formulating the Anambra State Green Yield Action Plan, exploring policy and governance reforms, and securing the economic viability of these goals.

### Assessing the State of Anambra's Forests

The first step toward adapting green and sustainable yield goals is a meticulous assessment of the current state of Anambra's forests. This assessment should encompass several crucial dimensions:

Forest Health: Understanding the ecological health of Anambra's forests is paramount. This includes evaluating biodiversity, ecosystem services, and the impact of climate change.

Economic Utilization: Assessing the current economic utilization of forest resources is vital. This involves examining the types and volumes of forest products harvested, their economic value, and the sustainability of these practices.

Community Engagement: Gauging the level of engagement and benefit-sharing with forest-dependent communities is essential. It helps identify areas of improvement in community involvement and empowerment.

Legal and Governance Frameworks: Evaluating the existing legal and governance frameworks is critical. This assessment should include an examination of forest policies, regulations, and enforcement mechanisms.

### The Anambra State Green Yield Action Plan

Once a comprehensive assessment is complete, the next step is to formulate an Anambra State Green Yield Action Plan. This plan should be a detailed roadmap outlining the specific steps and strategies to achieve green and sustainable yield goals in Anambra's forests. Key components may include:

Sustainable Harvest Levels: Determining the maximum allowable harvest levels that do not jeopardize the long-term health of forests.

Biodiversity Conservation: Outlining strategies for preserving and enhancing biodiversity within Anambra's forests.

Community Engagement: Defining mechanisms to involve and empower local communities in forest management and benefit-sharing.

Policy Reforms: Identifying necessary policy and regulatory reforms to align with green and sustainable yield goals.

## Policy and Governance Reforms

Policy and governance reforms are integral to the successful adaptation of green and sustainable yield goals in Anambra State. Reforms may include:

Legal Frameworks: Strengthening legal frameworks related to forest management, including regulations on harvesting, land use, and community rights.

Community Participation: Enabling greater participation of local communities in decision-making processes and benefit-sharing arrangements.

Enforcement Mechanisms: Enhancing enforcement mechanisms to combat illegal logging and other unsustainable practices.

## Economic Viability and Green Yield

Ensuring the economic viability of green and sustainable yield goals is crucial. Strategies may include:

Value-Added Products: Encouraging the development of value-added forest products to enhance economic returns.

Diversification: Promoting the diversification of livelihoods for forest-dependent communities, reducing reliance solely on forest resources.

Eco-Tourism: Exploring opportunities for ecotourism and sustainable tourism practices within forested areas.

In this chapter, we've laid the foundation for adapting green and sustainable yield goals to Anambra State's forests. This journey requires a thorough understanding of the current state of forests, a robust action plan, policy and governance reforms, and a focus on economic viability. With dedication and collaboration, Anambra State can embrace green and sustainable yield, ensuring that its forests thrive for generations to come.

CHAPTER 17

**Measuring Progress toward Green and Sustainable Yield Goals**

The pursuit of green and sustainable yield goals demands not only commitment but also a means to measure progress effectively. In this chapter, we delve into the essential components of measuring progress toward these goals, including the development of green yield indicators, socioeconomic metrics, and the adaptation of technology for monitoring.

**Developing Green Yield Indicators**

Measuring progress toward green and sustainable yield goals necessitates the development of precise and reliable green yield indicators. These indicators should encompass various aspects, including:

Harvest Levels: Indicators should track the volume and type of forest products harvested, ensuring they remain within sustainable limits.

Ecosystem Health: Monitoring indicators should assess the ecological health of forests, measuring biodiversity, carbon sequestration, and the maintenance of ecosystem services.

Community Well-being: Socioeconomic indicators should gauge the well-being of forest-dependent communities, considering income levels, employment opportunities, and benefit-sharing mechanisms.

Legal Compliance: Indicators should evaluate adherence to forest management laws and regulations, particularly related to sustainable practices and community involvement.

**Socioeconomic Metrics**

Sustainable forestry practices extend their impact beyond ecological factors to socioeconomic dimensions. Metrics for assessing socioeconomic progress toward green and sustainable yield goals may include:

Income Levels: Tracking the income generated from forest-related activities, both at the individual and community levels.

Employment Opportunities: Measuring the number of jobs created by sustainable forest management practices and their distribution among local communities.

Education and Training: Assessing the availability and effectiveness of education and training programs related to sustainable forestry practices.

Community Empowerment: Monitoring the extent to which local communities are actively engaged in decision-making processes and benefit-sharing arrangements.

**Adapting Technology for Monitoring**

In the modern age, technology plays a pivotal role in monitoring progress toward green and sustainable yield goals. The adaptation of technology is essential for accurate and efficient assessment. Technologies and methods include:

Remote Sensing: Leveraging remote sensing technologies such as Light Detection and Ranging (LiDAR), Synthetic Aperture Radar (SAR), and multispectral sensors to monitor forest characteristics at various scales, from individual stands to landscapes.

Geographic Information Systems (GIS): Utilizing GIS for spatial data analysis, mapping, and monitoring of forest changes over time.

Data Analytics: Applying advanced data analytics techniques to process and interpret large datasets, extracting meaningful insights for decision-making.

Digital Platforms: Developing digital platforms and applications that enable real-time data collection, reporting, and analysis, facilitating collaboration and transparency.

Community Engagement Tools: Employing technology to engage forest-dependent communities in monitoring efforts, enhancing their participation and providing them with a voice in decision-making.

The role of technology in measuring progress toward green and sustainable yield goals cannot be overstated. By harnessing the power of technology, we can achieve greater accuracy, efficiency, and transparency in our efforts to ensure that forests are managed sustainably.

In this chapter, we've explored the multifaceted approach to measuring progress. Developing green yield indicators, assessing socioeconomic metrics, and embracing technology are essential components of this ongoing journey toward sustainable forestry practices.

CHAPTER 18

## Envisioning a Greener Future

As we conclude our journey through the intricate tapestry of sustainable forest management in Anambra State, it is imperative to cast our gaze forward and envision a greener, more sustainable future. This chapter explores the long-term vision for Anambra State's forests, the enduring legacy of sustainable forest management, and the potential for Anambra State to serve as a model for green yield in Nigeria and beyond.

## The Long-Term Vision for Anambra State's Forests

Sustainable forest management extends far beyond immediate gains; it embodies a long-term vision that seeks to ensure the well-being of present and future generations. The long-term vision for Anambra State's forests encompasses several vital elements:

Ecosystem Health: A thriving forest ecosystem that supports biodiversity, carbon sequestration, and ecosystem services while resisting the impacts of climate change.

Socioeconomic Prosperity: Forest-dependent communities empowered with sustainable livelihoods, decent incomes, and a strong connection to their natural heritage.

Environmental Stewardship: Vigilant guardianship of forests, ensuring their protection, restoration, and resilience against external threats.

Cultural Resilience: The preservation and celebration of cultural values and traditions tied to forests, fostering a sense of identity and pride.

Education and Awareness: Ongoing environmental education and awareness campaigns that instill a deep understanding of the vital role of forests in sustaining life.

## The Legacy of Sustainable Forest Management

The legacy of sustainable forest management in Anambra State will transcend generations, leaving an indelible mark on the landscape and the people. This legacy encompasses:

Forest Regeneration: The renewal and expansion of forests, restoring their health and vitality.

Sustainable Livelihoods: Prosperous communities whose well-being is intrinsically linked to the sustainable use of forest resources.

Biodiversity Conservation: A rich tapestry of flora and fauna thriving within protected forests, including rare and endemic species.

Climate Resilience: Forests that serve as bulwarks against the adverse effects of climate change, moderating local climates and preventing soil erosion.

Cultural Richness: A cultural heritage deeply intertwined with forests, celebrating the symbiotic relationship between people and nature.

## The Potential for Anambra State to Serve as a Model for Green Yield

Anambra State as the "light of the nation" has the potential to shine as a beacon of sustainable forest management not only within Nigeria but also on the global stage. Its unique blend of ecological diversity, cultural richness, and pressing environmental challenges positions it as a model for green yield. Key elements that can elevate Anambra State to this esteemed status include:

Innovative Solutions: Pioneering innovative solutions that balance ecological, economic, and social objectives in sustainable forest management.

Community Engagement: Actively engaging forest-dependent communities in decision-making processes and benefit-sharing arrangements, fostering a sense of ownership and responsibility.

Policy and Governance Reforms: Implementing robust policy and governance reforms that ensure the effective management and protection of forest resources.

Education and Awareness: Continuing to invest in education and awareness campaigns that inspire a culture of forest conservation and environmental stewardship.

Cross-Sectoral Collaboration: Collaborating across sectors to leverage the potential of forests in areas such as tourism, agriculture, and climate resilience.

The potential of Anambra State to serve as a model for green yield lies in its commitment to a sustainable future, a future where forests stand as vibrant symbols of life, resilience, and hope.

In this final chapter, we have embarked on a journey of vision and aspiration. Anambra State's forests hold within them the promise of a greener, more sustainable future, and it is our collective responsibility to nurture and protect that promise for generations to come.

CHAPTER 19

## Conclusion and Call to Action

In the heart of Anambra State's lush landscapes, we have embarked on a journey through the realms of green and sustainable yield, envisioning a future where forests stand as guardians of life, prosperity, and hope. As we conclude this exploration, we recap the concepts of green and sustainable yield, underline their significance for Anambra State's forests, and issue a resounding call to action for all stakeholders to embrace and implement these practices for the preservation and management of this vital natural resource.

## Recap of Green and Sustainable Yield Concepts

Green yield, as we have discovered, represents the amount of forest products and services that can be harvested or used without compromising the ecological integrity and resilience of the forest ecosystem. Sustainable yield, on the other hand, denotes the quantity of forest products and services that can be harvested or utilized while simultaneously fulfilling the social, economic, and environmental needs of present and future generations. These concepts underscore the intricate balance between human interests and ecological imperatives, weaving a tapestry of coexistence between people and nature.

## The Significance of Adopting Green Yield Goals for Anambra State's Forests

For Anambra State, adopting green yield goals carries profound significance. It signifies a commitment to conserving biodiversity, enhancing ecosystem services, mitigating climate change, and supporting local livelihoods. It charts a course toward a future where forests are not mere resources to be exploited but thriving ecosystems that enrich the lives of its people.

The adoption of green yield goals also positions Anambra State as a leader in sustainable forest management, setting an example for Nigeria and the world. It showcases the potential for harmonious coexistence between economic prosperity and environmental preservation.

## A Call to Action for All Stakeholders

In closing, we issue a clarion call to action that resonates across all sectors of society. This call extends to the government, the private sector, civil society, and the local communities whose destinies are intertwined with Anambra State's forests.

Embrace and Implement Green and Sustainable Yield Practices: Let us embrace and implement green and sustainable yield practices as the cornerstone of our forest management efforts. This requires a comprehensive and holistic approach that integrates scientific research, policy formulation, capacity building, awareness raising, monitoring and evaluation, and the rigorous enforcement of forest laws and regulations.

Collaboration and Participation: Let us forge alliances across sectors and engage in participatory processes that ensure the voices of local communities are heard, respected, and integrated into forest management decisions.

Scientific Research: Let us invest in scientific research that deepens our understanding of Anambra State's forests, their unique ecosystems, and their potential for sustainable use.

Policy Formulation: Let us craft robust policies and governance frameworks that uphold the principles of green and sustainable yield, ensuring that our forest resources are conserved and nurtured for future generations.

Capacity Building: Let us empower individuals and organizations with the knowledge and skills required to implement green and sustainable yield practices effectively.

Awareness Raising: Let us embark on awareness campaigns that educate and inspire our fellow citizens to become stewards of our forests, fostering a culture of conservation.

Monitoring and Evaluation: Let us establish mechanisms for the continuous monitoring and evaluation of our forest management practices, ensuring that we stay on course toward a greener future.

Enforcement: Let us enforce forest laws and regulations rigorously, holding accountable those who seek to exploit our forests beyond sustainable limits.

By answering this call to action collectively and resolutely, Anambra State can ensure that its forests remain a source of wealth, health, and happiness for its people and the planet. The journey toward a greener future has begun, and it is a journey we embark upon together—a journey of hope, resilience, and enduring commitment to the harmonious coexistence of people and nature.

## Epilogue

The official slogan of Anambra State, "Light of the Nation," mirrors the state's visionary aspiration to be a prominent center of socioeconomic progress and advancement not only within Nigeria but also across the African continent. This slogan serves as a testament to the state's accomplishments in diverse sectors, including education, healthcare, agriculture, commerce, and security. Adopted by the state government in 2006, during the tenure of Governor Peter Obi, it encapsulates Anambra's journey towards becoming a beacon of development and growth.

In the context of this book, we introduce a modified slogan that resonates with the central theme: "Anambra State: Where Green and Sustainable Forests Are Home to All." This revised slogan underscores a critical message – that Anambra State's forests are not merely a valuable resource but a collective habitat for all its residents. It underscores the utmost significance of preserving and managing these forests in an ecologically responsible manner, ensuring their continuous provision of essential benefits for the well-being and prosperity of both current and future generations.

This slogan seamlessly connects the inclusive ethos of "Light of the Nation" with a call to action, emphasizing the imperative of green and sustainable forest management. It serves as a reminder of the shared responsibility among the people of Anambra State to safeguard these natural treasures, ensuring they thrive and benefit everyone who calls Anambra State their home.

It stands as a poignant reminder of the collective duty entrusted to the people of Anambra State, to protect these invaluable natural treasures, fostering their prosperity and ensuring they continue to enrich the lives of all who proudly call Anambra State their home.

Through the diligent effort of sustaining these forests, Anambra State will persist as the radiant "Light of the Nation." In much the same way that plants, through the miracle of photosynthesis, harness the power of light to sustain our world, Anambra State's commitment to sustainable forests serves as a beacon of hope and vitality for both its citizens and the nation as a whole.

## Additional resources for further reading.

If you are interested in learning more about sustainable forest management and green yield, here are some additional resources for further reading:

[Sustainable Forest Management Toolbox]: This is a website that provides a collection of tools, best practices, examples, and information sources to support SFM implementation. It covers topics such as forest policy, governance, planning, monitoring, assessment, reporting, financing, and education.

[Green Yield Report 2020]: This is a report that presents the results of a global assessment of green yield from forests. It provides data and analysis on the status, trends, drivers, and impacts of green yield at different scales. It also identifies challenges and opportunities for enhancing green yield and its contribution to sustainable development.

[Forest Ecosystem Services: A Cornerstone for the Green Economy]: This is a publication that explores the concept and value of forest ecosystem services. It illustrates how forest ecosystem services can support the transition to a green economy by providing benefits such as climate regulation, water provision, soil protection, biodiversity conservation, recreation, and health.

[Non-Timber Forest Products: A Review of the Contribution of Biodiversity to Human Well-Being]: This is a publication that reviews the role and importance of NTFPs for human well-being. It examines the diversity, availability, use, trade, and management of NTFPs. It also discusses the challenges and opportunities for NTFPs in relation to conservation, livelihoods, food security, and health.

## Glossary

1. Sustainable Forestry: The practice of managing forests in a way that meets the current needs for forest products while ensuring their long-term health and viability for future generations.

2. Forest Reserves: Designated areas of land that are legally protected and managed for the conservation and sustainable utilization of forest resources. They are critical for biodiversity conservation and sustainable forest management.

3. Forest Governance: The rules, institutions, processes, and practices that shape how forests are managed, including policies, regulations, and decision-making structures.

4. Forest Policy: A set of objectives, principles, and instruments that guide forest management. Forest policies provide a framework for sustainable forest management.

5. Community-Based Forest Management (CBFM): An approach that involves the participation and empowerment of local communities in forest management activities. It recognizes the role of indigenous knowledge and local communities in forest conservation.

6. Non-Timber Forest Products (NTFPs): Products derived from forests other than timber, such as fruits, nuts, honey, medicinal plants, and bushmeat. They play a crucial role in the livelihoods and nutrition of many communities.

7. Ecosystem Services: The benefits that ecosystems, including forests, provide to society, such as carbon sequestration, water regulation, soil protection, and biodiversity conservation.

8. Biorefineries: Facilities that convert biomass, including forest biomass, into various bio-based products such as biofuels, bioplastics, and biopharmaceuticals. They promote the use of renewable resources and reduce greenhouse gas emissions.

9. Carbon Sequestration: The process of capturing and storing carbon dioxide (CO2) from the atmosphere, primarily by plants and trees, which helps mitigate climate change by reducing CO2 levels.

10. Circular Economy: An economic model that aims to minimize waste and make the most of resources by reusing, recycling, and regenerating products and materials.

11. Indigenous Knowledge: Local and traditional knowledge passed down from generation to generation within a community or culture. It often includes wisdom related to natural resource management and ecosystems.

12. Bioeconomy: The production and use of biological resources, processes, and principles to provide goods and services across various

economic sectors. It emphasizes sustainability and the utilization of renewable resources.

13. Governor Charles Soludo: The current governor of Anambra State, Nigeria, known for his background as a former governor of the Central Bank of Nigeria and his efforts to promote sustainable forest management and environmental initiatives in the state.

14. Anambra Green Project: An initiative aimed at planting 10 million trees across Anambra State to combat deforestation, erosion, flooding, and climate change while improving livelihoods.

15. Sustainable Forest Management (SFM): The practice of managing forests to meet ecological, economic, and social objectives while conserving biodiversity and ecosystem integrity.

16. Agroforestry: A land-use system that combines tree cultivation with agricultural crops or livestock, promoting sustainability and diversifying income sources.

17. Photosynthesis: The process by which green plants, using sunlight, convert carbon dioxide and water into glucose (a form of sugar) and oxygen, releasing oxygen into the atmosphere and providing energy for the plant's growth.

18. Stakeholder Participation: Involving all relevant parties, including local communities, industry, government, and NGOs, in decision-making processes related to forest management.

19. Monitoring and Evaluation: Ongoing assessment of forest health, sustainability progress, and the effectiveness of management practices.

20. Partnerships: Collaborative efforts between different organizations, sectors, and stakeholders to address complex forest conservation and management challenges.

21. Green Economy: An economic system that aims to promote sustainability by reducing environmental risks and ecological scarcities while ensuring economic growth and improving human well-being.

22. Sustainable Development Goals (SDGs): A set of global goals adopted by the United Nations to address various social, economic, and environmental challenges, including those related to forests and biodiversity.

These terms encompass key concepts related to forest management, sustainability, and environmental initiatives discussed in the book.

# REFERENCE

Books and Articles:

1. David O. Edu, Etelbert E. Ayang, Agba D. O. Otonkue, & Bernard Enya Edu. (2010). Forest Resources Management for Sustainable Development in Cross River State of Nigeria: Challenges of the 21st Century. SSRN.

2. Adebayo Oluwole Eludoyin & Olamide Olaleye Iyanda. (2019). Land cover change and forest management strategies in Ife nature reserve, Nigeria. Springer.

3. Pius Adeniyi. (2014). Ensuring Environmental Sustainability Through Forestry in Nigeria. IJSER.

4. Oluwafemi Akinola & Olusegun Adekunle. (2018). Forest Conservation and Sustainability in Nigeria: A Case Study of Oban Hills Forest Reserve. LAP LAMBERT Academic Publishing.

5. Uwem E. Ite & Emmanuel U. Akpan-Idiok. (2016). Forest Governance and Sustainable Development: The Case of Nigeria's Cross River State Community Forests. Routledge.

6. Philimon Ng'andwe, Jacob Mwitwa, Ambayeba Muimba-Kankolongo, & Thomson Kalinda. (2015). Forest Policy, Economics, and Markets in Zambia. Elsevier.

7. Christian Okechukwu Ali, Chukwuma Okechukwu Nwafor, & Chukwuma Mac-Franklin Okeke. (2018). Forest Management Practices for Conservation of Threatened Plants: The Case of Gnetum africanum

(Welw.) C.DC., Gnetaceae in Anambra State, Nigeria. Journal of Forestry Research.

8. Uzoamaka Rita Onyeizugbe, Valerie Nnodu, & Alom Anselem Chukwuma. (2020). The Role of Forests on Climate Change Mitigation: A Case Study of Anambra State. International Journal of Environment and Climate Change.

9. Egbuche C.T., Anyanwu J.C., Amaku G.E., Onwuagba S.M., Duruora J.O., Nwachukwu C.U., Nnoli M.C., Nwachukwu I.N., Uzoma C.C., Okoro C.A., Nwachukwu M.O., Onyekuru S.O., Nnabuife E.L.C., Ukaegbu V.U., Okonkwo C.J., Umeokechukwu E.F., Okoye A.C., Onyia V.N., Ezealor A.U., Okoli P.I., Ugwoke F.O., Ezeonyejiaku C.D., Nnabude P.C., Okonkwo S.N., Ezeokoli O.T., Nwosu L.C., & Ogbu F.N. (2015). Assessment of Forest Resources Exploitation: Implication for Biodiversity Conservation. Journal of Environmental Science, Toxicology and Food Technology.

Online Resources:

10. FAO in Nigeria. (n.d.). Nigeria at a glance. Retrieved from [FAO](https://www.fao.org/nigeria/fao-in-nigeria/nigeria-at-a-glance/en/).

11. UN-REDD Programme. (2021). The role of forests in a green economy transformation in Africa. Retrieved from [UN-REDD Programme](https://www.un-redd.org/sites/default/files/2021-10/Forests%20in%20Green%20Economy%20in%20Africa-ENGLISH%20full%20report%20%28421614%29.pdf).

12. United Nations. (2021). The Global Forest Goals Report 2021. Retrieved from [United Nations](https://www.un.org/esa/forests/wp-content/uploads/2021/04/Global-Forest-Goals-Report-2021.pdf).

Additional Sources:

13. Spatial Distribution of Ecotourism Resources in Anambra State: A Nearest Neighbour Analysis Approach. Retrieved from [ResearchGate](https://www.researchgate.net/profile/Odum-Chigozie/publication/326292612_Spatial_Distribution_of_Ecotourism_R esources_in_Anambra_State_A_Nearest_Neighbour_Analysis_Approach/ links/5b4437feaca2728a0d68b0d0/Spatial-Distribution-of-Ecotourism-Resources-in-Anambra-State-A-Nearest-Neighbour-Analysis-Approach.pdf).

14. Anambra forest reserves are disappearing, but nobody cares. Retrieved from [ICIR Nigeria](https://www.icirnigeria.org/anambra-forest-reserves-are-disappearing-but-nobody-cares/).

15. Conservation of forest resources by rural farmers in Anambra State. Retrieved from [African Journals Online](https://www.ajol.info/index.php/jae/article/download/110471/100 211).

16. Forestry Research Institute of Nigeria. Retrieved from [FRIN](https://frin.gov.ng/).

17. Nigeria launches National Forest Policy – Voice of Nigeria. Retrieved from [Voice of Nigeria](https://von.gov.ng/nigeria-launches-national-forest-policy/).

18. Sustainable forest management practices: a viable panacea to the challenges of climate change in Nigeria. Retrieved from [FFPS](https://www.ffps.org.ng/docs/conf/sustainable_forest_manageme nt_practices_a_viable_panacea_to_the_challenges_of_climate_change_in _v_nigeria.pdf).

# About the Author

Evaristus Chukwugoziem Okonkwo's life journey began in the vibrant town of Nnewi in the Nnewi North Local Government Area of Anambra State, Nigeria. Born on the 10th of March, 1988, he brought with him a spirit of curiosity and determination that would shape his path in the years to come.

His educational voyage was a tapestry woven with diverse experiences. It commenced at Choice Nursery and Primary School, where the seeds of knowledge were sown. This foundation led him to Akamili Central School (Hill), continuing his educational ascent. Thriving on the thirst for learning, he embarked on a new chapter at Marist Comprehensive College Nteje, where his intellectual horizons expanded.

Evaristus's quest for knowledge knew no bounds, as evidenced by his pursuit of education at Summit International School. However, it was Abia State University Uturu that provided him with a profound academic home. Majoring in Environmental Resource Management, he delved into the intricacies of environmental stewardship—a theme that would resonate throughout his career.

His academic endeavors acted as a stepping stone to a career woven with diversity. The corridors of Airtel Nigeria welcomed him, exposing him to the dynamic world of telecommunications. The bustling environment of Mobil Service Station taught him valuable lessons in customer service and operational excellence. Amidst the vibrant landscapes of Cway Nigeria, he contributed to the realms of marketing and distribution.

In the present, Evaristus has found his purpose within the Anambra State Ministry of Environment, where he serves as the Onitsha Zonal Forest Officer. This role embodies his commitment to environmental conservation—a testament to his dedication, resilience, and a profound connection to his community.

Beyond his professional endeavours, Evaristus Chukwugoziem Okonkwo is defined by his devotion to family. His life partner, Mrs. Chinenye Juliet Okonkwo, shares in his dreams, supporting him through every endeavour. Together, they have been blessed with the joy of parenthood, nurturing their children and imparting values that enrich their lives.

Evaristus's journey embodies his role as a seeker of knowledge, a guardian of the environment, and a proud contributor to his community.

With each step, he embraces the lessons of the past while forging ahead with aspirations for the future. His voyage is one of inspiration—a testament to the transformative power of determination, unity, and an unyielding commitment to growth. This is his second book.